"In Wings for Val: Memoir of a Young Female Pilot, the authors are a group of students inspired by the life of pilot Valerie 'Val' Cappelaere Delaney to write in first person to tell her story and thus the origin story of the foundation bearing her name, Wings for Val. This book is like a pep talk from a big sister to young readers who are navigating life's ups and downs as they mature and contemplate their choices and dreams. Throughout, the book asks readers to think about the lessons and experiences Val is sharing and apply them in their own lives. The story is an excellent and profound way to showcase the continuing impact of one young Navy pilot's life as an inspiration to young people to fly high in their own achievements."

**Erin Miller**
Granddaughter of a Women Airforce Service Pilot (WASP), attorney, author of *Final Flight Final Fight* and *What Grandma Did*

---

"A heartfelt story for anyone working to overcome obstacles in pursuit of high-flying goals. Val shares her flightpath with insightful prompts to help you navigate your path. This book is a must read for those looking for inspiration from a true female warrior. Val motivates me to never stop pursuing my dreams and to always live life to the fullest. Val has your six!"

**Lt Col Vanessa "Siren" Mahan,** U.S. Air Force F-15E Strike Eagle & EA-6B Prowler Aircrew

"Valerie Cappelaere Delaney's life was short, but her legacy of achievement, leadership and heroism lives on through the Wings for Val Foundation. Enjoy this journey through her joys, challenges, difficult choices and ultimate sacrifice, in her voice as heard by those who knew and loved her best."

**R. D. Kardon**, pilot and author of FLYGIRL and ANGEL FLIGHT.

---

"This book is no doubt a massive undertaking of love and brave vulnerability that is guided by Val's intense and dedicated spirit to serve her county. Val confronted all the various challenges that were thrown to her with faith and grace with her family by her side - every step of the way. Whenever I see a feather on the ground or a V contrail in the sky, I will always remember Val's insatiable drive to serve her country and those around her. Sharing Val's story through the pages of this book will inspire every age reader who is looking for guidance and wisdom on life's journey. Her closing advice to "Live life to the fullest" is heartfelt and rings true for anyone."

**Kelly Murphy**, Director of Communications for Women in Aviation International

# Wings for Val

Memoir of a Young Female Pilot

**VALERIE CAPPELAERE DELANEY**
Edited by Barbara Jacobs and Jim Hoffmann

**Wings for Val: Memoir of a Young Female Pilot**
Copyright© 2022, Wings for Val Foundation
All rights reserved.

No portion of this book may be reproduced by mechanical, photographic, or electronic process, nor may it be stored in a retrieval system, transmitted in any form or otherwise be copied for public use or private use without written permission of the copyright owner.

It is sold with the understanding that the publisher and the individual authors are not engaged in the rendering of psychologic, legal, accounting, or other professional advice. The content and views in each chapter are the sole expression and opinion of its author and not necessarily the views of Fig Factor Media, LLC.

For more information, contact:

Fig Factor Media, LLC | www.figfactormedia.com

Cover Design by DG Marco Álvarez
Layout by LDG Juan Manuel Serna Rosales

Cover Photo Credit: Portrait by Phil Taylor, American Fallen Soldier Project. All rights reserved. Used with permission.

*Printed in the United States of America*

**ISBN: 978-1-957058-82-5**
**Library of Congress Control Number: 2022914728**

# CONTENTS

Dedication ................................................................. vi
Foreword .................................................................. vii
Editor's Note ............................................................. xiv

**PART 1: VAL'S STORY** ............................................. 1
   Introduction ........................................................ 2

**CHAPTER 1**
   Aviation Pre-Flight: My Childhood 1986 - 2000 ................. 5
**CHAPTER 2**
   Basic Instruments: My High School Years 2000-2005 ...... 19
**CHAPTER 3**
   Formation Flight: My Naval Academy Years 2005-2009 ... 31
**CHAPTER 4**
   Precision Aerobatics: My Flight Training 2009-2012 ......... 65
**CHAPTER 5**
   Low-Level Mission: Check Six 2013 ..................................... 87

**VAL'S PHOTO GALLERY** .......................................... 97

**PART 2: VAL'S LEGACY** ........................................... 117

**CHAPTER 6**
   Debrief: Adapt and Overcome ............................................ 119
**CHAPTER 7**
Wings Take Flight: How Does Val Inspire You? ..................... 131

Afterword by Destry S. Jacobs, 2d Lt., USAF ........................... 135
Acknowledgments .................................................................. 138
About the Wings for Val Foundation ........................................ 140
Sources ................................................................................... 142

# DEDICATION

This book honors US Navy Lieutenant Valerie Cappelaere Delaney. Through her stories, other young people will feel inspired to employ Val's "adapt and overcome" motto by connecting hard work and persistence with their biggest life goals (the bigger the better!), be they in the field of aviation or elsewhere.

Proceeds from this book will fund pilot scholarships for women through the Wings for Val Foundation (www.wingsforval.org) and raise awareness for the foundation. To that aim, we dedicate this labor of love.

# FOREWORD

This book began with a high school field trip to the 30th Annual International Women in Aviation Conference sponsored by Women in Aviation International (WAI) in Long Beach, California. At 6 a.m., five high school girls and I, Barbara Jacobs, climbed into a district van and headed out for a smooth two-hour drive to the Long Beach Convention Center.

It was a crisp, cloudless, sunny Saturday morning on March 16, 2019, and it was one of those days that was perfect for an early-morning drive. We each had some water and snacks for the travel duration.

The district van of young ladies and I were from Shadow Ridge School, Hesperia, California. We were looking forward to an exciting introduction to aviation through the Girls in Aviation educational program (ages seven to eighteen), a side event being held in conjunction with the WAI conference.

My adult daughter, Destry Jacobs, an aviation major, aviation enthusiast, and event volunteer, along with Gabriella Palmas, an American Airlines flight attendant and student commercial pilot, had recommended the student program. The two young ladies graciously volleyed back and forth between my group of high school students and their duties to the event. These women became a base for my students to field questions and forge friendships with.

My young students were amazed with the transparent and welcoming aura of all they encountered. They truly felt overwhelmingly awed, yet included. (Years later, two of these students would marry men in the military and both stated the events of this field trip helped them relate to their future husbands.)

The highly active events of the day sadly ended. We settled into the van and checked traffic. As fate would have it, the Cajon Pass (15 Freeway corridor to the High Desert) was closed due to a fire. There was no point in heading home right away; we'd only be sitting on the freeway for several hours. The students were thrilled.

With our time extended, it was back to the safety and convenience of the Long Beach Convention Center. My group was afforded a second opportunity to peruse the conference exhibition hall until it closed.

The girls were enchanted with additional time to investigate the plethora of variable aviation careers, and they were immersed in meeting and conversing with successful, competent, and trailblazing women. The wonders didn't stop there.

This one-day visit transformed into a passionate pursuit of "more." That "more" started after I stopped at a booth for the Wings for Val Foundation.

I liked the logo. Although I understood the logo to be wings, it looked like the word EVE in capital letters without the vertical lines on the capital Es. This foundation wasn't about selling or hiring. It was about advancing women! I was riveted.

Aside of this gold-lettered EVE wing-looking logo was a photo of a mesmerizing female aviator: confident, glowing with pride, and sporting an infectious smile. She had kind, inviting eyes. Her neatly tied-back light-colored hair, probably in a military bun, had a few loose strands blowing backward from an obviously strong wind.

She seemed at ease and delighted to be on the flight line, smiling . . . directly at me. I felt her. Oh no, this was a memorial organization! I was immediately struck low. This unknown woman reminded me of my precious daughter who was only about ten feet away with my students. Who was this young woman?

I started a conversation with a lady at the booth. I learned that from the trauma of the unimaginable loss of this lovely young woman arose an organization to champion others on. This EVE was touching lives. Her name is Valerie Cappelaere Delaney. I bought a T-shirt, magnet, and a colorful children's durable cardboard book. That book sits on my desk in my classroom at work today. But just who was this woman? What was her story?

As I turned the pages of the children's book, I caught a view of my students actively engaged in conversations at other booths. They were completely and utterly entrenched in the world of aviation wonder and discovery that was vibrant and alive right in front of them. That is what this Wings for Val Foundation does too.

The Wings for Val Foundation is not hiring or selling. It is inspiring and supporting, not to gain but to give, and I wanted more of that for my crew. I needed to introduce Wings for Val to my students.

With one of my own twins in the military and the other

military bound, both Air Force, the loss of a child is palpable. But isn't that true for any child? And what about this child, Valerie? She lives on in those EVE wings. Did you catch the "V" in the middle of the wings? "V" for Valerie. It is also known in nature for the support birds acquire and provide to each other as they fly long distances, such as with migration. So, with that V and logo and the support the organization provides, Valerie is still taking flight.

However, just having been introduced to Valerie Cappelaere Delaney, I still know nothing of her. The picture of her is mesmerizing. It imbues how she must have felt to be on the flight line: energized, vibrant, alive. I feel connected to her smile. I feel her calling to me with her eyes. There is a request, an almost silent pleading to make something happen.

Then, the idea tapped me on the shoulder, or perhaps she did.

I returned to the booth and nonchalantly asked the young woman there if it would be possible for my English students to write a book about the young Navy pilot's life journey. As I waited for the right person for me to pitch my rapidly forming idea to, another woman arrived. I was introduced to Valerie's mother, Doreen Cappelaere! With that introduction, I notified my students of our next Creative Writing project, and the electrical vibrance of this book project began. We did not know what we were in for.

My Creative Writing students sent questionnaires to family, friends, and colleagues of Navy Lieutenant Valerie Cappelaere Delaney. Then, an associate of mine, Jim Hoffmann (a history teacher, historian, and author), sorted through every responded word and spent weeks outlining the book with questions for students to research. A passionate research and cross-curriculum collaboration ensued.

Answering those questions allowed pairs of students to write about specific life events while other students worked on other parts. This kept the text chronologically organized. However, even with this outline and jump start, this book project was far more massive than any of us had anticipated. Perhaps because we wanted to do Valerie justice and perhaps because the loss of Valerie was still raw to those close to her, some conversations were painfully delicate.

School quarter and semester deadlines passed, student writers graduated, school courses and pacing plans changed, and then COVID-19 forced all public education into online distance learning and essential academics only.

The start of the 2020–2021 academic year found Shadow Ridge School in 100 percent distance learning and then 2021–2022 the school remained in virtual learning. As a result, I took over a portion of the completion efforts of Val's memoir. The final stages of the book were turned over to Jim Hoffmann, who shifted it to first person point of view. This lens brought Val's voice to the manuscript.

Soon Valerie became so familiar to Jim and me that

she became Val, a friend. Finally, the text was sent to family, friends, and additional colleagues to add, extend, and correct any errors in the text.

The finished product is a massive undertaking of love and brave vulnerability. Every hour, minute, second, word, phrase, paragraph, and personal memory devoted to this book was given freely and without financial compensation to any contributor.

This book belongs to the Wings for Val Foundation. Our hope is that the pages herewith fly with inspiration. Val was born to serve. She confronted challenges to serve. She even transcended the unimaginable to "adapt and overcome" in order to continue to serve. *If you let Val, she will serve you too.*

I thank Val's sisters, Allison Righter and Caroline Desroches, and the entire Cappelaere family for their courage to forge an organization that Val smiles upon. The organization is so like Val: young, vibrant, and with a purpose.

In creating the Wings for Val Foundation, the family has captured the essence of their beloved daughter, sister, sibling, wife, friend. With their sacrifice and forethought, Val continues to positively touch the lives of future generations with a legacy of support through their annual scholarship awards.

Thank you, Doreen Cappelaere, for tirelessly working with Jim and me. To the entire Cappelaere and Delaney families, Val's friends and comrades, the world is a better place because you are in it, and because Val is still in it. God bless, and may the organization continue to prosper through the gifts of Val and the organization's leadership for decades to come.

Valerie, I hope this book does your inside beauty justice. May you always live on.

## Barbara Jacobs, Teacher
Shadow Ridge School,
Hesperia, California

*The Wings for Val booth at the International Women in Aviation Conference, Saturday, March 16, 2019. Back row: Barbara Jacobs, Andrea Phipps, Becky Watson, Anne Bania, Cecilia Paizs, and Jenny Moore; Front row: Shadow Ridge Students: Miranda Agapay Bejarano, Amy Bojorquez Reel, Luzaurora Maldonado, Citlali Cruz, and Cynthia Smith (not shown). (Photo courtesy of Barbara Jacobs.)*

*Destry Jacobs and Doreen Cappelaere, Val's mother at the Wings for Val booth 2019. (Photo credit: Destry Jacobs.)*

# EDITOR'S NOTE

**Dear Reader:**

This work was primarily researched, organized, and written by the Shadow Ridge School Arts and Media Program in Hesperia, California, for the Wings for Val Foundation in awe and honor of one of our heroes, Lieutenant Valerie Alice Cappelaere Delaney. All proceeds go to support the Wings for Val Foundation and its fundamental mission and vision: inspire future young females to the greatest heights in aviation ever achieved, but also to simply "adapt and overcome" in whatever endeavors they take on in life.

Lieutenant Valerie Cappelaere Delaney *did not write this book nor sit for interviews. She had long passed before its conceptualization and final creation.*

Please understand that from the Introduction of this work through Chapter V, you will read as if Val herself is speaking. Wings for Val and the editors felt that this story, which will potentially impact thousands of young women, is too important to be told in the third person. It needed to come straight from Val's lips to your ears . . . albeit in a fictional sense.

However, this introduction and these five chapters were pieced together through extensive research: interviews, news articles, conversations with her family, and personal letters. We wanted to set down more than her life story, we wanted you to feel her heart and her pain and, ultimately, her encouragement that only she could give to you herself. We wanted to not only honor Val, but have you meet her!

We also feel this is what she would have wanted—not a book just about her, but rather from her. She would have loved to have personally met you.

While we've fact-checked beyond the call of duty and made sure every line was reviewed by those closest to her, we have taken a bit of literary license. Like all artists, the chapters by Val are our interpretation of what she would have said. They may not be exact. But they are enough and, as she would tell you: "Sometimes you just have to go for it!"

We did go for it. We did it for Val and we did it for you, dear reader, so you could have every reason and nothing standing in your way of reaching your bigger-is-better goals.

After reading this book, we have no doubt you will "adapt and overcome." It's a phrase you'll hear a lot in this book. Now Val's motto belongs to you. Take it as she shares with you her story…

**WINGS FOR VAL:** MEMOIR OF A YOUNG FEMALE PILOT

# Part 1
# VAL'S STORY

# INTRODUCTION

It's "Mom" signing in. It's strange, almost funny, but my friends and Navy comrades called me by this moniker—which became my "call sign" when I flew Navy aircraft. I guess it really did fit me, though.

I know what you're thinking: You're a young girl in this seemingly crazy world. I've been there. Yes, I have. By the way, I'm Lieutenant Valerie Cappelaere Delaney, US Navy pilot. The kind of pilot like in the movie, *Top Gun*. Well, close to that, anyway. I could go on, but how did I get there? It wasn't a walk in the park.

You know, even though I was my papa's girl and had a nice suburban upbringing in Maryland, I've experienced a lot in my life—the good and the bad. Nothing came easy.

I don't like to brag, but I was extremely smart and a great student. But truth be told, I wasn't always that way. Rather, I made myself that way. If I wanted to achieve something, I worked *really hard* to earn it. That, my sisters, is the key to success. For example, I worked with a math tutor so that I could take Advanced Placement Calculus in high school. It was important to me to understand the concepts and get an "A" in it. But life for me was a strife before that too.

From late elementary school to early middle school, I was short, overweight, and wore glasses. Let me tell you, I was teased mercilessly by the other kids, bullies mostly. These were hard times for me, and I struggled. So I faced the problem head on. I physically worked out as much as I

## PART 1: VAL'S STORY

could—daily at times. By my freshman year of high school, I had grown several inches and shed my baby fat.

Yep. This "pushing back" against the negatives in my life led me to feel a bit like a rebel, at least in the beginning; I wanted to tear things up. Both physically and mentally tough, I said what was on my mind and did not mince words.

I became so determined and set the very highest goals for myself. Again, I'm not bragging, but I was beautiful . . . fashionable . . . bought lots of clothes, yet I did not think for one second that I was all that.

You see, when you reach your goals in life, it's very important to make sure you are extremely kind and generous, and perhaps most important, spiritual, faithful, and always grateful to God and your family. I mean, who can truly do anything alone?

Even though I did some pretty crazy things in high school (and even got in trouble for some of them), I'm proud to say that I, Lieutenant Valerie Cappelaere Delaney, never let my academics suffer. Ever. It took me until I got older to figure out why I became a rebel.

You see, that's not how young girls are supposed to be and act in this so-called modern world, but *I did*. And our world is changing somewhat, maybe . . . if just a little.

So, do you feel this way sometimes, too—lost, lonely, without a sense of direction? Think about it, for us girls, there are only so many role models: aviator Amelia Earhart, physicist and chemist Marie Curie, former First Lady Eleanor Roosevelt . . . You know what? Just chill. Let me tell you my story . . . because this ugly duckling turned herself into a beautiful swan inside and out. And you can, too!

**WINGS FOR VAL: MEMOIR OF A YOUNG FEMALE PILOT**

PART 1: VAL'S STORY

## Chapter 1

# AVIATION PRE-FLIGHT: MY CHILDHOOD (1986-2000)

---

*Valerie – A name of French origin, means brave, strong, and fearless.*

I was born Valerie Alice Cappelaere at Shady Grove Adventist Hospital in Rockville, Maryland, on May 14, 1986. I was the second baby girl to be born into the family of Doreen and Patrice Cappelaere. Eventually I was the middle child of three independent and competitive daughters, and I grew up in this close-knit family.

My two loving sisters, Caroline and Allison, provided

some hefty sibling rivalry. I learned from them to give as good as I got. I suppose that's where I developed my sense of struggle and perseverance. I made sure I was noticed.

I had an enviably strong relationship with my sisters. I called my elder sister, Caroline, several endearing nicknames over the years, from "Sis" to "Care" (which actually originated during Caroline's college years) to "Hey girl!"—particularly during phone calls. Ever wonder what others, family, friends, enemies, have to say about you? Well, I sure do! Besides, I cannot tell my story all by myself. So what about my sisters?

Caroline has a lot to say about me: "Val was my younger sister, born two years after me. We fought quite a bit growing up, but only because we were so close in age and did so much together. We were always in competition growing up. We played on the varsity soccer team together for two years in high school and always fought over clothes, because we wore the same size then too. We grew a lot closer once I moved out and went to college, and Val became one of my very best friends and biggest supporters in helping me cope with the loss of my infant son in 2011."

Caroline also noted a key personality trait about me, as you will soon see: I'm a rebel. "Val was wild growing up, always breaking the rules and pushing the limits. She was incredibly strong-willed," said Caroline Desroches.

For my younger sister, Allison, I would occasionally use names like "Alli" or "A-Dawg." In turn, Allison dubbed me "Valber." Hey, I kind of liked that name. It was catchy: "Valber." Do you have a nickname?

Allison has a lot to say about me too. "Val was my big

## CHAPTER 1
## AVIATION PRE-FLIGHT: MY CHILDHOOD (1986–2000)

sister, and we were very close. I looked up to her and admired her strength, tenacity, and drive. We had a fun, teasing, and playful relationship . . . and she always looked out for me," said Allison Righter.

Now, in life, I believe everyone needs someone or something other than family to anchor their soul to, somewhat like a lightning rod protects a building from dangerous storms . . . to be grounded for sanity's sake. For me? This was my church.

I'm proud to say that I was baptized and raised in the Episcopal Church. In fact, when I entered the Navy, determined to completely focus on serving our beloved nation, I relied heavily on my love of Jesus Christ, prayer, and the Bible. I eventually became a spiritual warrior for my family and friends in need.

My mom, Doreen Cappelaere, has a lot to say about me also. "Val is my middle daughter. We had a great relationship that was very close and mutually supportive . . . When Val was born . . . she popped out like a champagne cork and was ready to live her life to the fullest!"

From a very young age, I was musically inclined. I am not boasting, but from what I've been told (granted, from people who love and respect me), I had a beautiful singing voice and would break out in song at unexpected times. Singing centers me. Do you have something you are good at that centers you? I just love a good tune.

When I was about six years old, at a family reunion on the banks of the Potomac River, I recklessly picked up a microphone. To everyone's amazement, I belted out the Star-

Spangled Banner, word for word. It was incredible! Everyone was held spellbound by the voice of this little girl—me! People boating out on the river stopped to listen. If only the television show, The Voice, had been around back then. (Yeah, right!) My first unpaid gig! Fact is, nobody could believe it was coming from me.

As a result, my parents tried to start me on piano lessons to help foster this potential musical talent. They were unsuccessful. I was stubborn and refused to play the ivories for the teacher. I cannot explain why. I just wasn't interested in musical keys.

Like a CEO who owns 90 percent of the company refusing to acquiesce with his board on a new direction to take, I would sit on the piano bench, my feet purposefully swinging back and forth, silent, with my hands in my lap. Oh, yes, and my embarrassed mother coaxing me, "Valerie, play the piano music you practiced for your teacher."

Yeah, right. "No," I replied.

My mom continued: "Valerie, the teacher cannot help guide you if you do not play what you rehearsed. This will help you play tunes you would like to sing to."

Nope. Nada. Zip. Zilch. Not a budge. I simply sat there. It's called being passive defiant. You see, the piano was not singing—actively or metaphorically. At least not through me. The piano was work I didn't ask for; singing was joyful and natural.

My parents finally gave in and dropped the piano lessons from my weekly schedule. Funny thing is that this is one of the first battles I recall ever winning against my parents, who at

## CHAPTER 1
### AVIATION PRE-FLIGHT: MY CHILDHOOD (1986–2000)

times seemed like the Rock of Gibraltar. They tried to give me the world, but I wanted the world on my own terms. I'm a bit of a rebel, remember? Well, that was only one battle.

In the end, though, my parents won the war. You see, I did love to sing, and gleefully focused on my vocal talent. I soon sang in the Howard County Gifted Children's Choir; Madrigals in high school; an elite girls' choir at the Northfield Mount Hermon School; the Women's Glee Club at the US Naval Academy; and with the acapella group, The Stowaways.

My late, sorely missed Nana, Carolyn Drake, noted this about my singing talent. I must admit, her words still make my eyes misty.

"Valerie was a talented singer; always singing, even as a toddler. In middle school, Val had a solo role in *The Wizard of Oz*—a standing ovation resulted. At her high school graduation, accompanied by only a piano, Val sang a solo, 'There You'll Be' by Faith Hill. There was another standing ovation . . . and not a dry eye in the stadium," said Carolyn.

Ah, yes, the many mosaic memories which friends and family constantly reap upon you as you try to reach a semblance of introspective sanity. Actually, I am grateful for their open praise.

My sister, Caroline, continues to embarrass me on this point. "Val had the voice of an angel [and] from a young age she was always musically inclined. My parents tried to start her in piano lessons to help foster that talent, but she refused to play for the teacher, and so we eventually stopped going . . . [Val] was always in special choirs that required auditions, and I think she may have done some voice coaching."

My mom, Doreen, likes to remind the world that I loved to sing, as well. I guess I can't argue with her. She still chats about me having "a beautiful singing voice and would break out in song at unexpected times." You know, *it is what it is.* Don't let your family's fawning over you get in the way of your humility. We all need to be praised once in a while, but don't let it go to your head. The wellspring of praise might as well originate from those who support you.

So, yeah, well, now you know that I liked to sing. Do you like to sing? What else are you like as a person? How would your family describe you? Since a mosaic by definition is "a picture made up of small tiles," let's not stop there. What else was I like as a kid?

Mom says that red was my favorite color. It is beautifully vibrant!

Papa says that I loved fried chicken so much as a spritely young lass that, "I would get so sick after eating too much of it." (BTW: I proudly called my dad "papa" out of respect to my roots. That's what French children call their fathers!)

Big sister, Caroline, says that I simply loved food. Her reasoning? "We grew up with a French father who adored good food . . . he instilled that love in us."

In an artistic sense, aside from food, I had quite the eye for stylish clothes and dressed in the very latest trends. Along with my sheer grit for facing a challenge, my raucous traits were seen in dyed hair and a tongue piercing. Yes, a tongue piercing! My wild side was still hungry, and it would be fed. My unique love of life would not, could not, back down. Your unique love of life will not, and should not, either.

My very dear friend, Erin Rawlick Delaney, mentioned

# CHAPTER 1
## AVIATION PRE-FLIGHT: MY CHILDHOOD (1986–2000)

that I found a simple pleasure in: "A pen and paper! She (Val) was always writing notes, letters, and journals, both to other people and for herself. She wrote notes and letters to me all the time and had a way of expressing herself so well through her letters and journals," Erin said.

You know, I forgot about my love of writing, if just for a nanosecond. But, I mean, it is such a simple thing in life. Please do not forget those simple pleasures. Before you know it, they're passé and yet, that is what life is all about, isn't it? I guess it's fitting that you are reading these words in this book about me, huh? You must know that it means the world to me that you are.

And then there was Rex, our beloved German Shepherd. There is simply no way you can talk about Valerie Cappelaere Delaney without mentioning my fur baby: my living, breathing security blanket. I mean, what greater love can one get than love and security from a furry family member, right?

Having Rex as the newest member of the family was not in the original plan. We hadn't even really talked about getting a dog before we did, but *it happened.* It happened on what was meant to be another ordinary Sunday.

"Come on, girls, let's not be late for church!" Mom exclaimed, holding little Allison. In a moment or two, we all climbed into the family car with papa in the driver's seat.

I was very young, maybe four or five years old. Near the end of the church service, the priest gave the big announcement. A stray German Shepherd dog was found wandering around the church grounds and was temporarily being cared for by the priest. He had already advertised for several days, but no one had come forth to claim the dog. The dog needed a permanent home, so the priest made an announcement to the congregation.

"As some of you are aware, a dog has recently found its way to our church grounds. He appears to be a healthy young German Shepherd with a good disposition and a kind nature. Being young, he is rambunctious and active, desperately desiring attention, love, and a permanent home. It is my hope that one of you might be able to foster this lost dog with a caring home," said the priest.

There was a deafening silence in church at that moment. The creaks of wood from the pews were unusually silent. The smell of the air was stiff due to the lack of breathing. If there had been crickets in the belfry, you would have heard them. It suddenly got warm.

With the congregation stuck on pause, little ol' Val, me, I knew my calling. Wouldn't you do the same? This German Shepherd needed a home and I had plenty of concerned, caring love to give. The time had arrived. Little me stood up and said with a booming voice, "We'll take him!" The awkward silence had been broken, a vow had been declared, and mom and papa simultaneously uttered a rather dumbfounded, "What?"

The pews seemed to creak with life and the congregation breathed a sigh of relief, releasing a rousing roll of laughter and delight at the little voice that so adamantly wanted to take in the unwanted dog and provide him with a loving home.

The attention of a hundred happy eyes looking at me was a cause for a smile. I could not help myself. I was

## CHAPTER 1
### AVIATION PRE-FLIGHT: MY CHILDHOOD (1986–2000)

pleased with my decision and ability to act for the benefit of a living being—animal or human—in need, but would the three sisters really go home from church today with a dog? Three little heads turned to look up at their parents.

Doreen and Patrice now had three little girls staring excitedly at them with huge puppy dog eyes. "Pleeease?!?"

The girls could hardly stay in their seats until the priest released the congregation and they could meet the needs-a-home animal. "God's lesson was not quite what I was expecting today," Patrice gently whispered to Doreen. And I was the one who rolled that seemingly huge boulder down the path.

Pulled by three excited and anxious young girls—"little engines that could"—the Cappelaere family went to meet Rex. It only took seconds. Once the three girls pounced upon the pooch, the debate about adopting the dog was over. The dog was an immediate hit, and the four rapidly bonded. It was obvious that this was meant to be. And to everyone's surprise, except mine, Rex then became an important member of the family.

Rex was our buddy. He was just as ready for play as he would be to listen to our delights and woes. When it was time for school, Rex would go to the bus stop with the three of us: Caroline, Allison, and me.

My papa enjoys recalling this part of my life. It . . . makes me gush a bit with pride and joy. "Rex was the best dog for the girls. He used to pull all of them on a sled in the winter and go to the school bus stop with them," Patrice said.

Big Sis, Caroline, remembers a little bit more detail. "Rex

was our first dog growing up . . . Our family hadn't even really talked about getting a dog, but Val popped up in the middle of the announcements and shouted, 'We want him!' We all laughed, but after church, we went to see if we could adopt him, and he became our dog from then on . . . My family had him for most of our childhood," Caroline said.

Little Sis, Allison, remembers even a bit more detail. "Rex was such a sweet, well-trained dog. We used to have him pull us in the wagon or on our rollerblades around the neighborhood, and he even helped rescue the three of us when we got stuck in ice down near a storm management drain while playing hockey in our backyard. He knew we needed help and went around front to get my mom, who was shoveling our driveway. He was our hero and such a sweet family dog, and Val absolutely adored him," Allison said.

Since no family story is complete without the mom's version, let's hear it. "Rex became the best dog for our family. He was so gentle and kind and was very protective of Val and her sisters. In the winter, he would pull the girls on their sled in the snow. We had Rex for about twelve years. We think he was two years old when we got him. It was a very sad day for our family when we had to have him put down," Doreen said.

Rex unconditionally loved me and my sisters. In turn, Rex's love taught us how to love each other *and ourselves*. He changed our lives for the better. Perhaps, you, too, have a pet which changed your life? How did this innocent creature make you a better person? I wish I could hear your story in person. Please share it with a loved one.

Yet, my life was no "bed of roses," as the old adage

# CHAPTER 1
## AVIATION PRE-FLIGHT: MY CHILDHOOD (1986–2000)

goes. I, too, struggled. Life is absolutely like a poker game, and I was dealt a bad hand sometimes. For example, and it's not easy to talk about because it still hurts, but I was bullied in school around the age of twelve.

The fact that I wore glasses and was overweight made things worse. (I'm sure my love of fried chicken didn't help. BTW: It's okay to laugh at yourself once in a while. This helps keep you healthy, sane, and centered.) However, I know now that *I was normal, and the bullies were abnormal.* It still emotionally hurt me back then.

But you know what? The taunts from those misguided individuals who had a false hate in their hearts— not love— and the resultant river of tears which flowed from the spigot of my soul ultimately helped to make me stronger. I had power for me.

The bullying I endured drove me to meet that challenge head on. I did whatever it took to succeed. At this point in life, I began to adapt in order to overcome my challenges, although I did not consciously recognize it at the time—the Marine motto: "adapt and overcome." This would affect me deeply when I grew older, as you'll soon see.

Being bullied isn't fun. The pain is real, but it can be a catalyst to change. As the great but fictional drama teacher, Mr. (William Michael) Schuester stated once in Glee, "A good nemesis only makes you better." (*Glee,* season 6, episode 5) At that moment in my life, I became determined, as you can, too, to defeat this negativity. I used it as a tool. I turned to my rebel nature . . . and started physical training . . . on my own!

As an aside, and which tends to go hand-in-hand with

being a rebel, I became daring and, at times, hung out and participated in a negative adolescent scene. I would soon learn that I needed to change my trajectory too. That scene was not going to get me where I wanted to go. My deep desire to play soccer helped me focus on improving my daily choices and physical fitness. My love for soccer sort of saved my life. I hope you have an activity in your life that you love being a part of. Nurture it.

Once I chose this physical path to redemption, a typical day would include the following colloquy. "I'm going jogging, Papa!" I would announce. Not waiting for a reply, I would bolt out the front door and down the driveway, rapidly disappearing into the distance. After the door closed, my father would say to my sister Caroline, "Again. She seems to always be out jogging."

Caroline would quickly reply, "She has a goal, Papa."

"I know, and I am proud of her," Papa would state plainly.

My papa, Patrice Cappelaere, perhaps my biggest cheerleader in the realm of sports (and food), corroborates this.

"She always picked the hardest route and never avoided a challenge. Val decided on her own to start jogging in the neighborhood, then become a soccer goalie. We had to take her to specialized goalie training camps. She eventually became a midfielder in high school and played on the same varsity team as her older sister," Patrice said.

Yes, this rebelliousness in me—to stand up to and counter negativity—started to bubble up and coalesce in my conscious mind. We all have this capability inside of us, you, me, everybody, regardless of race, color, or gender. I'm nothing special, just determined to succeed.

CHAPTER 1
AVIATION PRE-FLIGHT: MY CHILDHOOD (1986–2000)

My friend, Mia Stender, bless her heart, even noticed this trait in me. "Val was a rebel. I think she loved to do her own thing. I think she loved the thrill of being her own person," Mia said.

Naturally, those closest to me, my family members, noticed this rebelliousness too. My older sister, Caroline, said this about me: "I don't think life was easy for Val. There were always obstacles for her to overcome and I think that's why she adopted the [US Marine] motto 'adapt and overcome.' She was short, overweight, and wore glasses as a child, and so she was teased. Once she hit puberty, though, she grew tall, thinned out, and then she started wearing contacts and eventually got the PRK surgery [photorefractive keratectomy surgery which physically reshapes the eyeball] to become a pilot. She had struggles getting into the Naval Academy, and then she had to work incredibly hard to become a jet pilot *as a female in a predominantly male field* [editor's italics]."

Though for me, Valerie Cappelaere, I did not let gender discrimination stop me. And you should not either.

Even my dad noticed this internal and external struggle going on. Girls, I know many of you feel that your dad isn't paying too much attention to your struggles, but you'd be surprised at what they see and feel about their daughters.

"Val grew and started to work out so that by the time she entered high school, she made varsity soccer and lacrosse. Her life was extremely challenging and competitive, but Val always took the biggest, most difficult challenges," Patrice said.

I want to be clear on one particular point, though. Even though the bullying affected me when I was young, I acted upon it through physical training to fight back. Eventually I learned to not let what others think of me drag me down to the depths of despair. Remember what Glee's Mr. Schuester said about your nemesis—be it person, place, or thing: use the negativity to better yourself and do not believe what others say about you to be true. Only you know the truth. Truth has power, so be brave enough to harness that power—for the payoff is well worth it!

Caroline reflects this fact. Interestingly, though I was very caring and highly interpersonal, I cared little to none about social media. "She didn't care too much what other people thought about her. She had a few friends, but those friends she loved like family . . . Val didn't really have time to care about social media with everything else going on in her life. She was too busy most of the time," Caroline said.

PART 1: VAL'S STORY

## Chapter 2

# BASIC INSTRUMENTS: MY HIGH SCHOOL YEARS (2000-2005)

---

Now, to the standard, albeit sterile stuff. I grew up in Ellicott City, Maryland, a suburb some twenty miles west of Baltimore, and attended public schools in Howard County, Maryland, graduating from Centennial High School with high honors in 2004, and lettering in soccer and lacrosse.

I might add that my belief in myself and hard work paid off when I made the varsity soccer team as a *freshman no less!* Let me tell you, this was not easy to do.

I already mentioned above how my singing talents grew throughout my school years and beyond, from my days with the Howard County Gifted Children's Choir to The Stowaways during my Navy days. The point here is that I was part of a group of people who loved the same thing I did: singing. You, too, should seek out such groups. This helps provide pride in yourself for accomplishing something as well as the joy that comes from bonding in camaraderie, mutual support, and friendship.

Yet I am a rebel at heart and far from perfect, with a wild, mischievous side. I was always breaking the rules and pushing the limits. If a line was drawn, I'd test it. At times I would act before considering the consequences (like drinking alcohol with my soccer team before a school dance). It just seemed like a fun idea at the time; the consequences were not.

I soon realized my adolescent ideals were not creating the person whom I wanted to become. In fact, my lack of forethought at times was creating some big hurdles to overcome. I needed to turn things around. Have you ever felt this way about yourself?

To address the issue, I started journaling, soul searching, and self-reflecting. I soon understood that if I wanted to change, it would be through hard work. My hard work. I, not anybody else, had to do it. This self-action had to happen. And action is what I did!

In true Val style, I threw myself 100 percent into making up for lost time and opportunities. At the same time, I used that energy to pull others up with me. Yes, up, not down. I needed a positive vibe and productive tribe around me. So, besides soccer, lacrosse, and singing, I established SADD (Students Against Drinking and Drugs), a club at my high school.

I was finding my true self, shining a little light onto my most inner voice. When I look back, I can see the beginnings of my leadership skills starting to take shape. In the process, my caring nature also returned . . . and shined.

I was so laser focused on changing my life around within a short period of time that I shocked my friends when I told them one day that I wanted to serve our country in the US Navy! "Crazy Val!" bounced off the lips of my closest friends.

You see, while it's easy to be static, it's hard to change. My friends simply could not fathom such a radical departure from what they knew Valerie Cappelaere to be. I mean, come on, no one really expected me to give up my fashionable clothes and tongue ring for uniforms and officer mandates. In fact, my high school classmates even voted me "best hair" for my senior year. I'm sure my friends asked the rhetorical question on everyone's mind: "No way she would cut that off, would she?"

I suppose when my older sister moved away after high school, I started examining my life for what it really was. I tried to be real with myself. I had a profound appreciation for all I had been blessed with: family, home, opportunities.

I suddenly realized that the most significant successes are the ones that are the most challenging, the ones that are not easy but worth the effort (which means a sacrifice). As a result, I would have to sacrifice the old life and friends that were leading me astray.

I wanted to climb that mountain of success, metamorphosed through my vision. But I knew I had to do it alone—and quickly—to make up for lost time, that time that had no focus when I did not have a plan. I came to a somber realization that being a leader—and a trailblazer—is lonely, whether you have people cheering you on or not, which I certainly did through my loving family and friends. My heroes who blazed a path before me—Amelia Earhart, Marie Curie, and Eleanor Roosevelt—seemed to be whispering this in my ears.

As with many young people around my age in high school, my life radically changed after the attacks of September 11, 2001. It kind of woke me up from my wayward misdirections in my teen years. You see, I began to change almost immediately after this national tragic event. My mom, Doreen, recalls how much I had changed during this short time frame of my life.

"Valerie was very rebellious during high school, and my husband [Patrice] and I joked that she became the most reformed of our three daughters after graduating from the Naval Academy," Doreen said.

The US Naval Academy? I still cannot believe it, but it's true. Why such a dramatic shift in attitude—from rebel to soldier? You see, on Tuesday, September 11, 2001, I was inspired by the many sacrifices on that tragic day. It made me think of my many relatives and ancestors who had served our country before me. I, too, decided to serve our country—in the military.

My papa, Patrice, noted the moment I made this paradigm shift in myself. "It was during her junior year when

## PART 1: VAL'S STORY

she decided to try out a week at the academy to see if she would like it. The first few days were extremely hard, but then she completely loved the challenges and the camaraderie."

My mom noticed this paradigm shift, as well. "Val became interested in serving her country during high school. Her maternal grandfather, Colonel Richard Drake, US Air Force retired, had become ill and was moved to a nursing home near us in Catonsville, Maryland. Val and her sisters visited their grandpa almost every day after school, and Grandpa would come to our house on the weekends. Val spent a lot of time talking to him about his military career and being a pilot in World War II through the Vietnam War. I think these conversations sparked her interest. I was supportive of her wanting to serve her country," Doreen said.

This change was so profound, heck, even my older sister Caroline noticed it. "Val mentioned wanting to go to the Naval Academy during her junior or senior year of high school. I was completely shocked and surprised because she was the wildest child, always rebelling and getting into trouble, and I couldn't believe she would want to go to such a regimented and rigorous school. Val was so stubborn, though, so I knew if that's what she wanted then that's what she was going to do. There was no changing her mind. I probably did try to talk her out of it, but she wouldn't listen. We have multiple family members who have served, and I know she was strongly influenced by our grandfather, who was an Air Force pilot," Caroline said.

I cannot forget Allison's take on my change. "Val wrote about her decision to apply to USNA after experiencing our grandfather's funeral at Arlington National Cemetery shortly after 9/11. She loved hearing stories of other family members who had served in the military from our nana, including about our grandfather and great-uncle who were pilots. She inherited a strong sense of patriotism and wanted to serve our country and to be a part of something larger than herself. And I think it took a tremendous amount of God-given courage to knowingly commit to service during a time of war. I was very supportive of her attending the Naval Academy and loved visiting her often," Allison said.

So, it was about this time that I decided to stop messing around and start getting serious about my life. I went from a rebel without a cause to a rebel with a cause. Like my maternal grandfather, Colonel Richard Drake, US Air Force, I wanted to be a pilot in the military, but the Navy was my calling.

The summer before my senior year, I decided to attend a summer seminar at the Naval Academy. A week-long program, it prepared me for life at the Naval Academy. It was so lifelike, we were not treated with kid gloves but just like plebes, or first-year students. It was kind of like a boot camp for the military. Yeah, it was pretty tough.

This seminar was no picnic. But I was determined. My dad noted: "At first, Val didn't like it, but by the end of the week, she knew she wanted to attend USNA! Applying to the academy is extremely difficult, and Val took this very seriously."

My senior year (2004), I went through the arduous process of applying to the US Naval Academy. It was not easy, to say the least. I had to take a grueling physical exam, which included a timed run, various physical activities like pull-ups, sit-ups, and push-ups. But—and this was the scariest part—I also had to interview with our Maryland state senators and our representative to Congress, the late Elijah Cummings (Maryland's 7th congressional district). Thankfully, before these interviews I had decided that my tongue ring had to go and so I took it out and threw it away, never to want it again!

These were heady interviews, I can assure you. But these were the types of challenging hurdles we all must overcome in life. For me, the lesson I learned here was that it's easier to overcome difficult challenges when you are well prepared, which I made sure that I was.

And then, I hit a wall. My initial attempt to enter the US Naval Academy failed. I was crushed. As you learn in life, though, when you are knocked down, you have to get up off the ground, wash your face and comb your hair, and get back to it. It's really that simple. This was my temporary stasis when I graduated from Centennial High School in May 2004.

Olympian and WNBA star, Candace Parker, talks about this exact thing in an interview with Brittanie Fowler on SwishAppeal.com—how to overcome failure: "You know, there's obstacles in life, and it's about how you handle it. Sometimes it's not what happens, but rather your reaction to it," said Candace.

One of Candace Parker's idols, basketball star Michael Jordan, perhaps even one of the greatest athletes ever, also talks about how to overcome failure in an article written by Flavia Medrut on goalcast.com: "If you're trying to achieve, there will be roadblocks. I've had them; everybody has had them. But obstacles don't have to stop you. If you run into a wall, don't turn around and give up. Figure out how to climb it, go through it, or work around it."

Amelia Earhart said something similar many decades before Michael Jordan was even born. "The most difficult thing is the decision to act. The rest is merely tenacity. The fears are paper tigers. You can do anything you decide to do. You can act to change and control your life and the procedure. The process is its own reward," said Amelia Earhart.

Get the point? Today, you might think of the fictional *Avenger* series character, Captain Marvel in the 2019 film of the same name. There's a part in the film where Carol Danvers (Captain Marvel) remembers being knocked down at various ages in her life. Each time, however, she pulls herself back up. You see, whereas failure is when you stay down, success is when you get back up, learn from the mistakes, and try again. It's okay to fail. It is not okay to stay there or wallow in failure. That would make you a perpetual victim. You are more powerful than that. So get up and get to it!

Thankfully, due to the USNA Foundation Scholarship Program, I attended the Northfield Mount Hermon School, a private college prep school (with a student-to-teacher ratio of 6:1), to hone my physical and mental skills. Northfield Mount Hermon is a coeducational boarding school located in Mount Hermon, Massachusetts. It is a member of the Eight Schools Association, a group established in 1973 of private college-preparatory schools in the northeast United States. It was in this school that I completed a fifth year of high school before being admitted into the Naval Academy the following year. Remember, I had some time to make up for when I didn't have any focused goals.

My mom noted my determination. "Val did a postgraduate year of high school at the Northfield Mount Hermon School in Massachusetts and then was accepted the following year into the Naval Academy. This showed a lot of determination and perseverance because Val had applied to other great schools and had several acceptances that she could have taken. She knew she wanted to study engineering and she wanted to attend the Naval Academy!" Doreen said.

Yet my success, as with all people, is not purely self-created. We all rely on somebody sometime in our life for help and guidance. Some are family. Some are complete strangers—but for the Grace of God, they help us. Some people might call them guardian angels. Do you have one? Mine was Navy Captain John Craighill.

"I met Val as a possible Naval Academy candidate. I was always available to her and her parents as an advisor on the admissions process. During my naval career, I was on the staff of the Naval Academy and served on the academy admissions board in 1988. When she was not admitted on her first try for a Naval Academy appointment in 2004, I encouraged her to try again," John said.

Getting into the US Naval Academy was extremely challenging. In fact, in the beginning, it almost seemed impossible, but I did not lose sight of my dream, nor did I quit. Remember: a dream is just a dream if you do not act upon it to make it come true.

My older sister, Caroline, described this process perfectly. "Val did not have it easy in applying to the Naval Academy. We grew up in Maryland, which is one of the hardest states to get an appointment to the academy from. She had to meet with multiple government representatives in order to do so. Then her senior year she was caught drinking at a high school dance and was suspended from school for a few days . . . Val had to write letters to the academy and the government representatives to explain what had happened and how she had grown from the situation. She was eventually accepted to the academy but had to do a year of prep school at Northfield Mount Hermon before she could attend . . . She really didn't like it there, but she stuck with it and eventually got to the Naval Academy, where she really seemed to flourish in all she did, both academically and in all the extracurricular sports and activities."

I was far from perfect, and I morally atoned for the mistakes I made in my life. As forged aluminum created the bodies of the planes I flew, my mistakes forged my character, my womanhood, my soul. Mistakes are proof we are human. Without these mistakes, sometimes hard ones to boot, we would not learn. We need to reflect on our learning in order to grow. Period.

Show me a successful person in life, and I'll show you someone who screwed up a lot. It's that simple. The sapling of perfection can only sprout from the grafting of imperfections—not the other way around. It's against the natural order of the universe. Not to say at some point in life, I became wholly perfect like Jesus or Buddha. I didn't.

## PART 1: VAL'S STORY

I am just an imperfect woman who sought perfection through life's experiences. So, with God's love and grace, I graduated from Northfield Mount Hermon Prep School in May of 2005 and—like a jet on a carrier in an active theater of war—catapulted into my war of "good trouble."

> July 21, 2004
>
> Dear Mom,
>
> I just wanted to write you a little note to tell you I love you. Thank you for all of the things you do for me and the time you spend with me. I don't know how I could do all of the things I do without your help. I know it's not always easy to put up with me but you do it somehow.
>
> Mom, I'm going to miss you very much this next year. I will realize how spoiled I've been living at home and having you take care of me so well. I know sometimes you may not think this but you're an awesome mom and a hott momma. I am very lucky to be able to go to the gym with you and have you help me with my workouts. I don't know too many moms in better shape than you, really.
>
> Anyways, the best thing about you mom is how you do so much for others. You have constantly supported + encouraged me, my sisters, and papa in everything we do — trust me, we acknowledge the things you do + appreciate everything even if we don't show it sometimes. I hope you like what I picked out for you. You deserve to look great and have nice things just like us because you're awesome on the inside and out. I love you.
>
> Happy Birthday Mom! Love, Valerie

*A letter I wrote to my mom on her birthday on July 21, 2004.*
*(Courtesy of Doreen Cappelaere.)*

# WINGS FOR VAL: MEMOIR OF A YOUNG FEMALE PILOT

# Chapter 3

# FORMATION FLIGHT: MY NAVAL ACADEMY YEARS (2005-2009)

---

*"I am still the luckiest girl for having such a great family!"*
I wrote this on a card to my papa on September 8, 2005

**I MADE IT!**! I got into the US Naval Academy at Annapolis, Maryland. What a feat, if I may say so myself. I mean, little ol' Valerie Cappelaere, from little ol' Ellicott City, Maryland. I mean, who am I, and where the heck is that? I finally reached a mountaintop in my life, and girl, oh, girl, I was flying high, if but for a while.

My dear reader: You must remember though how arduous my journey was to get here. It's quite normal for people to readily recall the good times, the highest peaks of successes, but then forget about the lowest valleys of defeat.

Now, with life in the military, every day, every minute, and every second is laid out for you by your commanding officers, or COs. You are now the property of the US government. That "distant uncle" *owns you.*

Military life is very regimented, which, frankly, is not that bad. So, in honor of the military way of life, I will recount it month by month, year by year, for my existence at this juncture of life was like a clock with its minute and second hands spinning at Mach speed. But, oh, the memories.

## JUNE 29, 2005 - "I DAY"

I excitedly reported to the US Naval Academy for Induction Day, or I Day, for the projected Class of 2009 (the class date is specified by the class graduation year) and my first day of Plebe Summer. About 1,200 hopeful midshipmen—dubbed Fourth Class, or plebes, reported to I Day.

We were then rushed through various stations whereby our medical and dental records were formalized, paperwork signed, uniforms fitted, and of course . . . we received our obligatory military-style haircut. In fact, in preparation for this physical mutilation, my beautiful long hair was cut in a short stylish bob before reporting to the USNA for I Day.

Yeah, my trip to the big time wasn't easy: numerous applications; a multitude of nerve-racking interviews with important people like our state senators—but particularly the late honorable Congressman Elijah Cummings; my deeply painful rejected initial application to the hallowed halls of

## CHAPTER 3
## FORMATION FLIGHT: MY NAVAL ACADEMY YEARS (2005–2009)

the US Naval Academy; and my reluctant but necessary attendance at the Northfield Mount Hermon School.

I really had to put my motto into action. I made it and I became a better person because of this adversity, failure, rejection . . . *self-adapting and overcoming* became my new mantra.

To begin with, according to the Naval Academy, in a general sense, I Day is designed to "turn civilians into midshipmen," according to Wikipedia: Plebe Summer. Excitement dissipates once you're dropped off, though. I mean, it's saying your goodbyes quickly, followed by a generally emotional separation from your loved ones, followed by the old "Hurry up and wait!" routine coupled with having demands barked out at you. Most of I Day is one stand-at-attention line after another. No talking!

You get in line and wait at various stations for your assigned group, uniforms, medical records, salutation training, this mess hall, and these quarters . . . and, like I said, the obligatory haircut. Welcome to the US Navy. You are now a midshipmen 4th class—a plebe. Yep, some 1,200 of us marched to this process. We were ready, able, and devoted to our mission.

I became part of this well-oiled machine over a six-week period, a square peg in a round hole. Same clothes. Same manual ("Reef Points") to memorize. Same perfunctory salutations: "Sir, yes, sir!" or "Ma'am, yes, ma'am!" Same lack of sleep.

30 June 2005

Mom, Papa, Alli, Caroline + Neo,

I love you all very much! It is not too bad I guess after the fact, things we do aren't bad but while doing some things it's hard. I can just feel the sweat drip down my body when we have to stand in the hallways with our rifles, for example - and they are heavy. There are so many things to remember and specific things to do. Our company is cool. Our squad leaders are better than expected. It could be worse - as many things. We try to laugh it off and the girls in my room are working together well. John McCain is in my squad. He's nice but not overly friendly. Some other people are really helpful and friendly. My arms are bruised from getting blood drawn and I'm constantly sore. We had PEP for the first time, not bad. Tomorrow we get placed in ability groups after we take a test - I mile run, push ups + sit ups. I think I need to go. We never know what time or where we need to be places. I will write whenever I can. It's hard to sleep at night too.

Love so much,
Vaurie xoxo →

*Excerpt of a letter I wrote to my family on June 30, 2005. (Courtesy of the Cappelaere family.)*

## CHAPTER 3
## FORMATION FLIGHT: MY NAVAL ACADEMY YEARS (2005–2009)

As an important aside, the Navy has been trying to get more women and minorities into the ranks. Yes, there were several women in my class, not to mention minorities in general. Though stats for my Plebe Year (2005) are not readily accessible, stats for 2009 are: "Of the 1,230 incoming students, 435 are minority midshipmen or 35 percent, up from 28 percent last year," reported Aaron Morrison for the Associated Press.

In fact, the Navy has been trying really hard to expand the opportunities for inner-city minorities by opening up officer training to even people like me. Uncle Sam has finally realized that future recruits will more likely join the Navy, respond positively to officers, and be more likely stay in the Navy for the length of their career . . . if their officers look like them (gender and race). To be specific, "retired Captain Bernard Jackson, president of the National Naval Officers Association, states, 'To be able to see (yourself) in the organization [via officers of the same gender and race], it plays a strong part to have younger individuals stay,'" Aaron Morrison also reported.

Being a plebe, a first-year cadet in the Naval Academy, is about surviving the extreme mental, physical, spiritual, and emotional ups and downs of the training process. If you make it, you can move along in your military career to various pathways of service to our country, including the areas of naval aviation, special warfare, and the medical corps.

31 JUL 05

Mom Papa Alli + Caroline
 I enjoyed seeing you at church this morning. Alli — so many people said you looked beautiful. My good friend Logan Coffey a football player thought you were 22. Mom, you look great too — nice outfit! I love you all so much. I think we're in the "3rd phase" of training — they've lightened up a bit. Emily Lyren + Jenn Dunbar are my roommates now. We got a 48/50 on our Alpha inspection tonight — it was great. It's so cool that we are getting closer and closer to the end. It's unreal. Anyways, today was nice. Chaplain Baker told me I have a beautiful smile — I can't help it; seeing you all and Matt in church is such a nice end to every week. I am so lucky and thankful

*A letter I wrote to my family on July 31, 2005.*
*(Courtesy of the Cappelaere family.)*

## CHAPTER 3
## FORMATION FLIGHT: MY NAVAL ACADEMY YEARS (2005–2009)

> for where + who I am and all the people who love me. You guys are great :) I hope you took good care of Matt today. I wonder what you all did. Did Caroline get home safely? Did she get to meet Matt? I feel like I don't know what goes on but your letters help. And it would be hard even if we could talk for you to understand this place. But, I'm feeling awesome right now. Our company + squad are really coming together. I can't wait for you to meet everyone. I love you all. Another full week — the last <u>real</u> week.
>
> Love
> Valerie xoxo

*A letter I wrote to my family on July 31, 2005.*
*(Courtesy of the Cappelaere family.)*

Ma'am, yes, ma'am! The Naval Academy is strict. I know that some of you are thinking, "Yeah, the whole Navy thing sounds like it's no big deal—a joke." Let me tell you some cold, hard facts. Pay attention here, ladies and gentlemen, or the joke will be on you. Here is how Plebe Summer unfolds.

## INDUCTION DAY

Plebe Summer typically begins at the end of June or the beginning of July. Again, the first day is called Induction Day, or I-Day.

Upon the departure of our drop-off party, usually parents (who are then provided a presentation about Plebe Summer by the Naval Academy), we plebes are ushered into the front door of Alumni Hall, where we're greeted by detailers (upper-class trainers) who relish in training us to address them in the military cadence of "Sir, yes, sir!" or "Mam, yes, mam!" This salutation is known as a "sandwich."

Next, we receive our serial number, or "Alpha Number." This number will identify us for what will seem like an eternity while attending the US Naval Academy.

Our gear comes next: uniforms, combat boots, running shoes, and *Reef Points,* a plebe's Bible of sorts, which we must essentially memorize. It highlights the US Navy's mission, history, and traditions. Every sailor must know Reef Points by heart.

Then the obligatory haircuts: men are shaved bald, while women receive the "Plebe Chop," a chin-length cut. Interestingly, this haircut is no longer required in today's modern military.

## CHAPTER 3
## FORMATION FLIGHT: MY NAVAL ACADEMY YEARS (2005–2009)

Don't forget the slew of medical exams and vaccinations, which brings us to the back door of Alumni Hall. Here, we are taught proper saluting.

From here, we exit Alumni Hall and walk toward Bancroft Hall, our dorm for the four-year tenure of our stay at the academy. At this point, the Navy divides plebes into fifteen companies, known as Alpha Company through Papa Company (there is no J Company in the military). These companies will compete against one another. Each company is then divided into two platoons, with each platoon containing forty plebes. Each platoon is then subdivided into four squads, with each squad containing ten plebes.

The Oath of Office is held at 1800 hours (6 p.m.). It is public. We are sworn in by the Navy's commandant of midshipmen, and it is at that time that we officially become US Navy midshipmen!

Lastly, we are reintroduced to our trainers, or detailers, for Plebe Summer, and, alas, are yelled at the remainder of the night once we get back to Bancroft Hall.

## FIRST SET—TEAR DOWN

This is the first half of Plebe Summer, known as First Set. Its focus is to introduce us to military life in general. We take classes on Naval Leadership, Honor, Naval Warfare and Tactics, Rank Structure, and Unified Chain of Command. We must also memorize much of *Reef Points*, these bits of information which are known as "rates." The information entails knowing the ranks of the enlisted and officers in all branches of the military, memorizing NATO's phonetic alphabet, all

Navy and Marine ships and planes, as well as some uplifting quotes to promote positivity, or esprit de corps. Still think the whole Navy thing sounds like it's no big deal, a joke?

What is our daily schedule like? We have to follow what's called the Plan of the Day, activities which are all mandatory.

At 05:30 a.m., we are awoken from our slumbers by our detailers and populate a nearby athletic field, where we complete a daily Physical Education Program (PEP). We have to do calisthenics and a lengthy run.

Then we line up for meal formation, or attendance and uniform inspections en route to entering the dining hall to eat our morning chow. This is in front of Bancroft Hall for all the world to see, civilians included. What's interesting is we are questioned about our rates as we try rapidly to devour our food.

More physical activities follow throughout the day as per the Plan of the Day, as well as classes on naval practices. We also periodically work on marching in formation with our military-issued rifles, which is called a close order drill. And I have to tell you, military rifles are heavy to carry around everywhere.

Nightly, we are granted time to write letters home (about thirty minutes). Lastly, we sing the "Navy Blue and Gold" before mandatory lights out (21:45 military time or 9:45 p.m. civilian time).

## CHAPTER 3
## FORMATION FLIGHT: MY NAVAL ACADEMY YEARS (2005–2009)

> 11/17/05
> Sunday
>
> Mom Papa + Alli
> It's so exhausting here! This week has been really intense. We did a confidence/ropes course yesterday and the obstacle course a few days ago. I'm bruised + sore. I'm not sure if you know we have sports periods in the afternoons 4 times a week. I was doing intramural soccer which was fun but I talked w/ the inter colligiate sailing coach + said I could do sailing. We take out FJ's every day. Just 1 skipper + 1 crew. I do the crew part. It's hard but fun. I'm learning a lot + getting better at sailing. I have bruises on the sides of my legs from roll tacks - they are tricky. Anyways... I saw you and Coreen at the parade on Friday. I hope we looked ok?! I'm in the

*Excerpt of a letter I wrote to my family on November 17, 2005.*
*(Courtesy of the Cappelaere family.)*

## SECOND SET—BUILD UP

This is the second half of Plebe Summer, known as Second Set. Its focus is to turn us plebes into the Brigade of Midshipmen. We become polished Navy recruits during this process. We also are trained by a completely new set of detailers. What's really cool is that we get to attend special lectures (dubbed "Forrestal Lectures" after the first US Department of Defense Secretary James V. Forrestal) by such notable people as astronaut and Apollo 13 Commander Jim Lovell. These lectures give us a sense of pride in being midshipmen. Weekly marching parades in the town of Annapolis help us to develop our drilling skills. Where Plebe Summer ends, Plebe Year begins, the main difference being that we now have to add very challenging academic classes to our schedules.

## BRIGADE REFORM—A FULL BASE

The upper class, the rest of the Brigade of Midshipmen, return after Parents Weekend. This is called "reform formation" and is when the whole brigade is back and in their proper company areas. When these midshipmen return, the ratio of upper class to Plebes is 3:1. And here it gets quite interesting. You see, the upper class is instilled with the notion that they will help "teach" the plebes. What's the big deal, you ask? We plebes are now just second-class citizens in the Brigade of Midshipman. And these elder midshipmen remind you constantly by "sniping" you, that is verbally admonishing you if you screw up. Yep, anything in life worth pursuing will not be easy.

So, if you are serious about becoming a midshipman,

## CHAPTER 3
## FORMATION FLIGHT: MY NAVAL ACADEMY YEARS (2005-2009)

and wish to endure Plebe Summer, it is worth noting the following additional subtleties of this rite of passage if you want to join the US Naval Corps:

- More than likely, the next time you'll get to go home will not be until Thanksgiving;
- More than likely, your parents will not get to visit until after Plebe Summer.
- After Parents Weekend, when we plebes return to the yard on Sunday, there is an old naval tradition that you will be greeted by Christmas music wafting from the windows of "Mother B" (Bancroft Hall). This is a subtle (albeit cruel) reminder to us all that the next time you will get to go home will not be until the Christmas break;
- Right after Parents Weekend, you are issued computer access and can therefore start to communicate with home via emails;
- Thankfully, you are allowed a couple of phone calls during Plebe Summer;
- It's feasible to see your family, depending on leave, about every three months;
- If, for whatever reason, you are not able to get home for the holiday breaks, "sponsor families" are there to help provide those in need, as well as the academy's own King Hall, which provides a nice feast for those in need;
- When authorized, plebes get liberty to town on Saturdays (noon to midnight) but must stay within

- a twenty-two nautical mile circumference (25.3 regular miles) of the Naval Academy Chapel Dome, known as the "Twenty-two Mile Limit"; (US Naval Academy Parents' Club of Northern California); and
- Now *this* is interesting: if you have liberty to town, you may not be driven by anyone but parents, sponsors, or firsties (senior midshipman) . . . unless approved via a chit (special request to the company officer).

There you go...

## LATE AUGUST 2005

So began my freshman academic year (or Plebe Year) at the Naval Academy. Yes, I made my presence there at the academy purposeful and poignant. I wanted to make sure that I "made a dent in the universe," as the late Steve Jobs once said. Better yet, to quote Madam C. J. Walker, the first black millionaire, a female to boot, and a true pioneer and role model for us girls: "Don't sit down and wait for the opportunities to come. Get up and make them." And girl, I did!

It's been duly noted that I "earned an appointment to the US Naval Academy's Class of 2009, arriving at Annapolis as a member of 17th Company, and taking on the difficult major of Aerospace Engineering." (WingsForVal.org) Aerospace Engineering is a very challenging and expanding field, which I highly recommend you check out if you are interested in math, science, and creating new things. Now, all military

## CHAPTER 3
## FORMATION FLIGHT: MY NAVAL ACADEMY YEARS (2005-2009)

academies require students to also participate in a sport or club. Can you guess mine? I became a member of the Navy Women's Lacrosse Team. And remember that little voice thing I was good at? I also sang in the Women's Glee Club, as well as The Stowaways, a highly respected vocal group at the Naval Academy.

My baby sister, Allison Righter, as did my other family members and friends, found my success a bit incredulous. She said: "We joke that Val was the typical rebellious middle child who ended up becoming the most reformed after she started at Navy . . . So, she definitely . . . became more disciplined and started to grow in her confidence as a leader. She also really deepened her faith once she started at Navy and became an inspiration to me and countless others in this way."

Yes, my faith, my belief in God and Jesus, a higher power if you will—was vital to me. Do you have a belief in such a concept? If you believe life is precious—not random—how could life not be in control of a higher power?

The Bible and my ability to write were key components of my sanity and serenity while at the academy. Allison noted: "Her Bible [mattered most]. And maybe a journal to write in . . . During her time at the academy . . . Val really deepened her faith and held close to her Bible readings."

Interestingly, as I became more confident in myself, more in control, I ironically became more dependent on God. Sounds strange, I suppose. Is this true for you too? You would think the opposite would occur, right? More on this extremely significant development in my life later.

Another interesting development—what one might call a "God moment"—helped to guide me toward becoming a female fighter pilot in the US Navy. I was able to participate in a free flight lessons program at Lee Airport in Annapolis, Maryland. This was an incredible experience I will never forget. My mom, Doreen, excitedly noted this achievement in my life's flight path: "Val took her first solo flight in a small Cessna airplane from Annapolis, Maryland, to Cape May, New Jersey, and obtained her private pilot's license, all before graduating."

I loved flying and I loved the sport of lacrosse. I loved my teammates even more. The camaraderie we developed inspired me to no end. I mean, life is like a sport, if you think about it. It's about loving each other and helping each other to achieve success, to achieve great things.

Navy Coach Cindy Timchal said I was essentially a main cog in the team and helped to propel us from just a club team to Division I: Coach Timchal said, "We will always remember her strength of character and her passion as a lacrosse player," as reported by Caroline Darney in *Inside Lacrosse*.

In fact, my teammate and "girly" (think "buddy" or "bestie"), and naval aviator, Lieutenant Junior Grade Erin Rawlick Delaney, reminded me of how it was tough being a hardworking player, like me, but who did not necessarily see a lot of playing time, when our lacrosse squad went big time and joined the NCAA Division I competition. "She [me!] just really loved the team and loved lacrosse. It was very evident . . . That was the biggest thing she brought to the team. She always kept a good attitude and was always a leader throughout the transition," Erin said.

## CHAPTER 3
## FORMATION FLIGHT: MY NAVAL ACADEMY YEARS (2005-2009)

Yeah, "Er" (pronounced "air") and I had quite a bond through our love of lacrosse—and each other. "Like fingers in a glove," we stuck together, as the old adage goes.

"Val never called me by my full name. She called me 'Er' . . . I met her playing lacrosse wall ball during the first week of school immediately after my Plebe Summer at the Naval Academy, August of 2006," said Erin Rawlick Delaney.

Have you ever had a friend like Er, who just won't stop complimenting you? Bear in mind that whereas it's a good thing to hear you're great, it's a bad thing to truly believe it. In other words, don't let the periodic "speed of sound" compliments you get allow you to relax your commitment to excellence. Sometimes, however, you just gotta let your friends speak their minds.

"Val was my best friend and mentor throughout the Naval Academy and then throughout flight school. She is the main reason I selected Naval Aviation and became a pilot . . . Val was the most supportive friend: we went on adventures together, we shared our secrets, gave advice to each other, and she was always there for me when I needed her the most," said Erin Rawlick Delaney.

My other best girlfriend or "girly," Mia Stender, whom I first met during her Plebe Summer (July 2006) and became very special friends with (I called her "Mi"), added some more air to keep my ego afloat.

"Equal. Deep. Demonstrative. Unconditional. Joyful. We showed up for each other. We were the kind of friends you would have your whole life, without needing to be anything different than you are . . . in other words . . . There will be friends in your life for a time, and friends in your life forever. Val was special to me because our friendship was unassuming and natural—it was clear to both of us that we would know each other for a long time. That's not to say it was easy. Val challenged me to be my best self. If I was up to something she didn't approve of, I would know it! But she was kind and supportive in all the ways we knew how to be at the age that we had each other," said Mia Stender.

Mia showed me something really important in life: good friendship. Having friends per se is not the point. Having one or two truly good friends means everything. What makes a good friend, you ask? To quote Mia Stender: "Equal. Deep. Demonstrative. Unconditional. Joyful." If your friend does not treat you equally, does not care about you deeply, does not demonstrate love for you in a healthy way, does not love you *no matter what,* and does not bring joy to you—forget about it. It's not a true friendship. A good friend exhibits all of these qualities.

I want to share with you this little episode. Here's an example of good friends in action.

"We both broke up with our long-time boyfriends around the same time during my freshman year at USNA. We always checked in on each other and even got each other Valentine's Day presents that year! . . . She was fiercely loyal and . . . always checked in on me throughout flight school to make sure I was doing OK," said Erin Rawlick Delaney.

Mi reminded me of this little bit. It's a tad bit embarrassing, but nice to hear even so. "Throughout the transition from club to varsity lacrosse, Val wasn't receiving as much playing time.

## CHAPTER 3
## FORMATION FLIGHT: MY NAVAL ACADEMY YEARS (2005-2009)

She took it upon herself to find a significant role on the team, even if those contributions weren't as much on the field. She was the spirit of the team, always encouraged everyone, and acted as a team 'mom' of sorts," said Mia Stender.

Can you believe that? The team mom!

But the respect went both ways. As I told Er once in a letter: "I keep the support of our close lacrosse girlfriends with me always. I know you guys will carry me through."

Here's another example of good friends in action. Mi noted how I was able to take a negative and turn it into a positive.

"Val and I spent our share of time on the Navy Women's Lacrosse sideline, and sometimes at practice, the 'backup' squad would be relegated to the opposite side of the field to shrink the scrimmage groups," said Mia.

So . . . As a contorted Coach Timchal shouted, "I need to shrink the scrimmage groups! Backup squad, you are to go to the opposite side of the field!" . . . Mia headed on out to the far field and shouted toward me—who was already bounding her way— "Sent over to the outcast side today!"

I retorted, "Oh, Mi, isn't this the best day?"

Incredulous, Mi shouted, "What?"

I could not help myself. I was overjoyed. I shouted, "We get to practice together! I haven't spent enough time with you this week at all!"

Mia broke out into an unexpected laugh. "Val, you can find the silver lining in anything!"

"I love you too, Mi!" I exclaimed as I watched the scrimmage line move forward.

## LATE AUGUST 2006

At this point, I began my sophomore academic year (Youngster Year) at the academy. My second year, I had to develop—like a long-distance runner—that extra tough physical, emotional, and spiritual rhythm to make it through. The trick? I stayed as focused as possible on the tasks at hand and avoided shenanigans.

## SUMMER 2007

Things started to heat up by my second summer. I was selected for summer training on the *USS Cowpens,* a Navy guided missile cruiser. I had to fly by myself from Baltimore to Singapore, with layovers in San Francisco and Tokyo. I boarded the *USS Cowpens* in Singapore and set sail with the *USS Kitty Hawk* Battle Group.

Coincidingly, Sean (my future husband) was doing summer training on the *Kitty Hawk,* but even though we were in the same US Naval Academy class, we did not know each other yet.

The ships crossed the equator heading toward Australia and we midshipmen (Sean, me, and a few others) became "Shellbacks." Through a big Navy tradition, a ceremony was held in our honor on the ships. Frankly, it was a big deal and lots of fun.

Once we arrived at our destination, Perth, Australia, we were granted a few days of rest and relaxation, or R&R. It was here that Sean and I first met each other. In fact, on the flight home, we sat next to each other on the plane ride. It turns out that we both grew up in Maryland in counties next

## CHAPTER 3
## FORMATION FLIGHT: MY NAVAL ACADEMY YEARS (2005–2009)

to each other and were part of the same class at Navy (Class of 2009) but met in Australia! How strange life's connections can be sometimes.

You know, still, life at the academy was not exactly easy, as there were countless challenges I had to overcome. Consequently, in Summer 2007, during one of my training sessions with the US Marines at Quantico, Virginia, I formally adopted my life's motto: *adapt and overcome!* Although different, the US Marine Corps and US Navy both operate under the US Department of the Navy. Thus, the two military branches often integrate training and support. Naval Academy graduates can either enter the Marine Corps or the Navy. Thankfully, I was selected for Naval Aviation upon graduation.

It was during this critical time in my life that my mantra hit me like a tidal wave . . . *"adapt and overcome."*

My younger sister, Allison Righter, noticed this engulfing mantra. She said: "Val picked up that mantra ['adapt and overcome'] during one of her summer trainings while at Navy . . . during her Marine Corps rotation since that is adapted from a common Marine Corps slogan. I think when she heard it, it resonated so much with her, since that is really what she had already been doing for so long. And it really started to stick when it became an inside family joke when she totally overused it on our sisters' spring break trip to the Grand Canyon. So we jokingly said it to each other all the time, and I think it really did help center her . . . and keep her striving forward despite any obstacles or setbacks she had."

Let me continue this illustration of my mantra.

Allison and I already had hiked a distance to the start of the trail on the south side of the Grand Canyon when Allison went to take a drink of water from her camel pack.

"Val, there is something wrong with my camel pack, the water won't come out!" she exclaimed.

Without stopping, I replied, "Adapt and overcome, Alli!"

"Val, I'm not kidding. I want some water and it's not working."

"And Alli, I'm not kidding either, adapt and overcome! You have the water. We'll figure it out. We need to get moving, now!"

Allison, getting frustrated at this point, thought, What is her problem? *"Adapt and overcome" is not solving the fact that I can't get to my water.* I'm ready to push her off this ledge, and we haven't even started our trek . . ." A quick fantasy of Allison hurling me off the edge of the cliff flashed across Lil Sis's twisted mind. "Ugh!"

Hours later, Allison griped, "Val, my legs are getting tired, let's take a breather."

"Adapt and overcome, Alli! You can do it." Allison thought to herself, *I don't like you right now!*

Yep, I adopted this mantra, "adapt and overcome," like my life depended on it. In fact, no, my life *did depend on it*. Success is the goal of life, no? Further, you must dream to reach the stars, but a dream without action is just a dream. Success comes from having dreams with goals to meet those dreams, and a plan of action to carry through to your victory, whatever that is. My mom, Doreen Cappelaere, even noted this about me. "Val was never lost in her life! She always had plans and goals!"

## CHAPTER 3
## FORMATION FLIGHT: MY NAVAL ACADEMY YEARS (2005-2009)

As with any flight in life where you take off, you will not only experience different places and events, but many, many fine people. My life's flight path was no different.

I was a midshipman (the lowest rank in the Navy) in the beginning of my career. However, to expand my experiences and training opportunities, I enrolled in the Navy's Summer Internships for USNA Midshipman Program (four to six weeks in length) which is "intended to educate and inspire midshipmen by broadening their scholarship and leadership experiences, developing their critical thinking skills, and deepening their appreciation for practical applications of their academic studies," according to the US Naval Academy, Summer Internships.

Commander Jonathan Stevenson, who became my friend and mentor and oversaw my internship, noted my agility and astuteness when it came to handling . . . a vomiting child.

"When she was a midshipman intern at my command . . . she came to practice with the young girls (nine to eleven years old) on the lacrosse team. I was coaching girls, including my daughter. She provided them with an example of what they could become and left an indelible impression on both my daughters. After practice, we took her out to dinner and my younger daughter got sick right on the table after dinner. Val didn't even bat an eye and helped make my daughter feel better while we all cleaned up the mess. It wasn't an unusual occurrence for parents of three young kids, but it was an unbelievable show of composure for a twenty-two-year-old college student," said Jonathan.

Yep, even vomit will not deter me from doing my best.

You always have to look at the big picture. Is vomit important to me? No. Is my reaction to it important? Absolutely. Adapt and overcome.

Oh, yeah, in exchange for helping out Jon Stevenson's daughter's lacrosse team, my mentor took me on my first ride in a Navy jet—an F-18 fighter jet! It was exhilarating and I loved it!

## SEPTEMBER 2007

Amazingly, I began my junior year (called Second Class year) with study abroad in France during my first semester—at the famed Saint Cyr Military Academy!

Now, my French heritage, which I got from my father, Patrice Cappelaere, led me to quite an ambitious undertaking: Can you say, "Parlez-vous francais," . . . or "Merci beaucoup?" You see, I participated in this first-ever student exchange between the US Naval Academy and the French Military Academy, Saint Cyr, arriving on August 24, 2007, for essentially learning what you do not prefer—or expect—to learn in order to be a well-rounded warrior, aguerrissement.

The specialized French training, more or less pontificated by Napoleon himself way back when in 1802, according to Wikipedia: Saint-Cyr-l'École, included the standard lack of sanitation "going to the field" but also good grub and wine, Thursday night picnics, equitation duties, lack of a strict schedule, and even visits to historical sites.

This experience was totally cool for the most part. Besides, there is definitely something mystical about heading

## CHAPTER 3
## FORMATION FLIGHT: MY NAVAL ACADEMY YEARS (2005-2009)

back to the homeland of your ancestors. I mean, this is where YOU started as a person, as a part of the human family.

Here is the actual essay I wrote to the school to try and get accepted into this prestigious program. Frankly, I'm proud of my expressions, which I plodded out. It's one of the first times I actually was able to write what I truly felt. Have you ever written something like this?

---

**Valerie Cappelaere**
06 October 2006

### The Opportunity to Study Abroad

If American people did not study abroad in France, I would not exist today. My American mother grew up with an interest and love for the French language. She spent her entire junior year of college in France, completely immersed in the culture while studying in this foreign country. Eventually her efficiency with the language grew until she was able to hold natural conversations in French and meet people, more specifically, my father. My father moved to America, where he became completely immersed in the English language and started his own business. Today, my parents are fluent in both languages and my father is a successful businessman and engineer.

My dual cultural upbringing has significantly shaped who I am. Since a young age, I have enjoyed traveling to France and visiting my family there. I have been surrounded with French language, food, history, and culture since my birth, which has encouraged me to develop my proficiency in the language. To this day, I still face somewhat of a language barrier between my grandparents and cousins in France. It is only with each extended visit in France that I become more comfortable and more able to communicate with French people, and more importantly, my family. Traveling to and studying in France and being fully immersed in the culture will help me perfect my abilities for myself and for the tradition and heritage into which I have been born.

I immediately took an interest in the possibility of studying abroad in France. I am very excited and willing to accept the challenge of learning and studying in the French language. This opportunity would provide encouragement for me to communicate with others at the highest level. At the same time, I want to discover more of the military tradition of my father's family. Two of my French relatives attended the Saint Cyrienne School in France. My grandmother's cousin was a general in the Foreign Legion who graduated from St. Cyr and later taught there. In France, there is great honor and prestige given to students of this school. It would be an honor for me to study at St. Cyr or the Ecole Navale in France. I would be challenged on many levels, which would raise my language efficiency and bring me closer to my French heritage and family, especially now as my grandparents are becoming older.

I have a strong personal interest in continuing my study in the French language. It will be an important way for me to learn, not only how to speak better, but learn about myself and the tradition of my family. I admire the courage my mother had to leave her school and live in another country to study for a year. I only hope to follow in her footsteps to face the same challenges and develop my level of French skill and proficiency. I want to carry on the heritage I have grown up with to communicate with my family and to pass on the same tradition to my family in the future. It is equally as important to me as an American to continue learning about other cultures and different ways of life to develop myself for leadership. As a naval officer and as an American, I hope to develop relationships with people of many cultures and be able to work with an understanding of peoples' differences. I would accept this opportunity to study abroad with enthusiasm and as an outgoing and interested representative of the US Naval Academy and the United States of America.

I highly recommend a foreign exchange program, whatever your ethnic background. The trip could instill a sense of awe, wonderment, and pride—not only for yourself, but for your family members who came before you.

I will always remember landing on French soil for this challenging exchange program. It was a homecoming of sorts. My small step onto my ancestral soil was predicated upon the great leaps my ancestors took before me. Their struggles allowed me to be the strong person I became. How do you feel about this? What have your ancestors afforded you to do?

Surprisingly, this trip was not easy. I come from a very close-knit family, and a network of friends which I wholly cherish. Maybe you do too? The distance and isolation were tough. Remember this, though: Anything of value requires struggle. It's that simple. So, even though I enjoyed my trip to France, my friend, Mia Stender, noted the entire experience had its trials for me.

"Her time in France was hard. It was a dream of hers to live abroad, and she did it boldly—but it was a step away from a strict cadence toward graduation at USNA . . . the lacrosse team . . . from her community. It was not an experience without sacrifice. She overcame it the way she did everything, with a smile on her face. But she expressed vulnerability to her friends, to me. I think she learned she had to do that, to let people know she was struggling so that we could help her," said Mia.

## CHAPTER 3
## FORMATION FLIGHT: MY NAVAL ACADEMY YEARS (2005–2009)

> Papa, I have also loved discovering France + the French language and feel proud of where we come from + our French family. You're the best Papa! I love you and I won't forget to call you!
> Love, Valerie

*Excerpt of a card I wrote to my papa on June 21, 2009.*
*(Courtesy of Patrice Cappelaere.)*

## AUGUST/SEPTEMBER 2008

I began my senior year (called First Class year) at USNA. I was given many leadership positions in the Brigade of Midshipmen.

Spoiler alert! This is not to say that I was perfect at any point in my life, an angel. In fact, even at the academy, my mischievous side was known to occasionally peek through, like the time I smuggled some plebes in the trunk of my car to go see a concert. The convo went something like this . . .

"You want to go see the concert? I've got a plan," I proudly touted to the plebes, who looked up to me with googly eyes like the Greek goddess of war herself, Athena.

"Yes, Val! We really want to go. But how?" asked the two plebes. You see, they were restricted to the academy campus, or the Yard as it was called, at all times during their first year.

"Well," I conspired, "I'm going to drive my car over to the track, where the two of you can get into the trunk of my car. You will have to stay there until we are far from the front gates. Is that something you can do?"

"It is a good thing we are roommates with each other. Yes, we can do that," replied the plebes.

"Okay then," I replied. "Now, get going and I'll see you tonight."

The weather actually worked in our favor. When the time came to smuggle out the plebes, the moon was blocked by clouds. It was darker than usual, and it appeared that no one was at the track. As promised, a lone car crept forward to the parking lot. The crunch of the gravel grinding into the dirt was the only sound.

As the vehicle approached the north side of the track, two shadows appeared. I stopped my car and pulled the lever that unlatched the trunk. The shadows silently slunk in, and with a small cord I had placed there earlier, the shadows closed the trunk upon themselves. The shadows remained unseen.

I cunningly used my academy pass to exit the base and drove around the bend. Far from the view of the gate, I stopped the car and tapped the ceiling twice. I once again pulled the lever to unlatch the car's trunk. The plebes emerged and scurried into the back seat of the vehicle. Surprisingly it had been an easy ride.

"Thanks for the soft pillows and padding back there, Val. I can't believe we are really doing this! What a night this is going to be. Woohoo, Val! Let's go!" Though I am not proud of my deceptive behavior, which could have had serious

## CHAPTER 3
### FORMATION FLIGHT: MY NAVAL ACADEMY YEARS (2005–2009)

repercussions for all of us if we had been caught, it was a celestial night.

The good: On May 10, 2008, I was allowed to leave the academy to attend a special event. I sang at my older sister's wedding! It was joyously magical. However, getting to that point took a bit of effort.

Caroline noted: "When we were talking about what she should sing, we were in our parents' kitchen, and she kept coming up with all these country song suggestions which weren't my thing, and then jokingly asked if she should do an interpretive dance to go along with it—all the while demonstrating what she would do. It was hilarious. She ended up singing a Sade song without any interpretive dance."

*Excerpt of a card I wrote to my family on February 14, 2008.*
*(Courtesy of the Cappelaere family.)*

## MAY 22, 2009

I graduated and received my commission! In fact, my Commander in Chief, President Barack Obama, handed me my diploma: a Bachelor of Science degree in Aeronautical Engineering with a minor in French.

So, after four long and arduous years of mental, physical, and spiritual training, I earned it. "After four years at the Naval Academy, Val graduated in the top part of her class. She was also accepted for flight training because of her high standing and desire to achieve. The Naval Academy and training are not easy by any means, but Val took it in stride," said John Craighill.

Every year, about a thousand midshipmen graduate from the US Naval Academy, Annapolis, Maryland, and in May 2009, I did, too, as a member of 17th Company.

The best part was the notice I received of being selected to be a naval aviator. Sheer ecstasy! I was off to Navy Flight School. A goal and a dream combined.

As you probably already know, while life has its good, it also has its bad. It was not too long after this (in December 2009), that my mom, Doreen, became very sick. Let me tell you, right here and now, as you get older, and your love for your family and friends blooms, you come to realize that your life means nothing without them. You find that you would willingly sacrifice your own life for the health of your family and friends. It's natural if you're instilled with the eternal love and respect of a higher power.

Seeing my mom fight her personal battle with breast cancer turned my world upside down. Thankfully, God turned me right

## CHAPTER 3
## FORMATION FLIGHT: MY NAVAL ACADEMY YEARS (2005-2009)

side up. This turmoil led me to become an active warrior for spiritual matters with respect to my family and friends.

This was a "timeline moment" in my life—you know, if you were to chronologically list key events in your life—this was one. My mom's breast cancer scare was the moment where God truly made sense to me.

We all have a purpose in life: you, me, our families, friends, or people we've never met. For the first time in my life, I read the Bible with discernment, passion, and care. I prayed like there was no tomorrow, for my mom, my family, my friends, for strangers I never met, and for me, even. I knew I needed prayer as much as anyone. There is an old adage that goes like this: "Success fools smart people into thinking that they cannot do wrong." Just because I started to make inroads into making that dent in the universe, I still had a way to go.

**WINGS FOR** VAL: MEMOIR OF A YOUNG FEMALE PILOT

# Chapter 4

# PRECISION AEROBATICS: MY FLIGHT TRAINING (2009-2012)

---

**JUNE 2009**

At this point in my whirlwind naval experience, I reported to Aviation Preflight Indoctrination (API), which is basic flight training at Naval Air Station (NAS) Pensacola, Florida.

Er was there when I had been chosen for flight school. "She was excited to challenge herself, to take that next step . . . She's always been fearless," said Erin Rawlick Delaney.

My life was really picking up speed—supersonic even—at least, it felt like that. It's funny how when you are young, you want time to speed up, but when you are older, you want it to slow down. This entire period was just a blur, truthfully.

I was never bored. The Navy kept me busy and I kept myself busy. One thing I learned from overcoming obstacles in my life is that inaction made things worse for me both mentally and spiritually. Action is the key to a successful life.

The great Dale Carnegie, sales guru, author, and self-help pioneer said, "Inaction breeds doubt and fear. Action breeds confidence and courage. If you want to conquer fear, do not sit home and think about it. Go out and get busy," according to Shivam Agarwal, quoting Dale Carnegie.

I cannot help but laugh at that quote. I mean, that's me—Valerie Cappelaere—all the way.

My friend and mentor during my internship reminded me of some pointed conversations we had had about my desire to "Fly Navy."

"We talked a lot as she made her decision to go into naval aviation. As she went through flight school, we talked about the struggles of getting through the program, about being a female in a male-dominated profession, about just being a successful Navy pilot, about . . . [managing] her relationship with Sean and her relationship with the Navy," said Jonathan Stevenson.

# CHAPTER 4
## PRECISION AEROBATICS: MY FLIGHT TRAINING (2009–2012)

> September 2009
>
> Dear Papa,
>
> ...and have a happy birthday.
>
> I wish you a very happy birthday and lots of fun on your new boat. I think of you + mom often + I know you all are enjoying life together. I can't wait for you to visit me some time soon! I will be working really hard and thinking of you + the lessons and example of hard work you give to me. I love you Papa ♡ Valerie

*Excerpt of a card I wrote to my papa in September 2009. (Courtesy of Patrice Cappelaere.)*

## 2010

Next, I was sent to NAS Corpus Christi, Texas, where I flew the T-34C Turbo Mentor for primary flight training. And this is where I had another timeline moment, in all honesty. Only, this was also holy in its essence.

On Sunday, July 4, 2010, I gave a brief public confirmation of my life, and of my love and commitment to God, to my close-knit family, and to my country, in front of the congregation at St. Mark's Episcopal Church in Corpus Christi, Texas. I did this at the request of my friend and mentor, Father John Hardie, whose church I attended while at NAS Corpus Christi.

I do not want to bore you. Please understand that this public confirmation, a sermon if you will, really bubbled up from my soul, and I was so proud and honored to share my love of God and country on this national holiday. Who was Valerie Cappelaere? What did Valerie Cappelaere stand for? I am nervous, but here goes...

> **I would like to first start off by introducing myself.** My name is Valerie Cappelaere. I'm not sure if everyone here knows me by name, but I recognize a lot of your friendly faces. And to anyone who is new or visiting St. Mark's today, I would like to welcome you and let you know that this church is a special place where I have felt extremely welcomed since I came to Corpus last October. I consider this church my family away from my family. Being in the military causes me to

# CHAPTER 4
## PRECISION AEROBATICS: MY FLIGHT TRAINING (2009–2012)

move around quite often and it's a testament to the open and friendly atmosphere here that I feel able to speak and it's truly my pleasure to do so.

**I would like to start by offering a prayer.** Let us bow our heads: Dear heavenly Father, on this day of the anniversary of our country's independence, help us to be especially mindful of what it means to be free. Let the Holy Spirit open the minds and hearts of your people here today. Lord, I pray that this message fills your house with words that are acceptable to you and that bring glory to your holy name. Amen.

**The day of my first flight in a naval aircraft was the same day I missed a phone call from Father John.** In my present state of euphoria, I returned his call to learn that he wanted me to speak today in church. His request took me by surprise, sort of like my first takeoff in a T-34 earlier that day when my instructor gave me the controls and actually expected me to fly the plane! I thought over Father John's request, feeling extremely humbled by the opportunity to share a little bit of myself—something he believed would be meaningful to you. And like that first flight, I survived with God's help in the same way I was able to put together something to say and stand before you today to share it.

**I am the middle daughter of three girls; the stereotypical middle child you hear of was me, but probably worse.** I was rebellious and different, especially physically different looking than my two sisters and my peers. Often teased and chosen last in gym class, I was overweight, had glasses and braces. I realize now that my differences kindled my desire to be challenged. That young overweight girl lost 65 pounds and became a high school scholar-athlete. Though my physical appearance changed drastically, my rebellious spirit still needed lots of work. It took a few learning lessons for me to finally "get it." I eventually got suspended from school—I realized my lifestyle couldn't continue down the same path (the path many of my high school friends maintained in college and even to this day). That wasn't the life I was made for.

**My family has had several members serve in the military.** I've always enjoyed listening to my grandmother's stories of her father and brothers. One memory that particularly affected me as a teenager was my grandfather's funeral at Arlington National Cemetery. The thirty-seven years he served in the Air Force was honored at his gravesite facing the gaping hole in the

# CHAPTER 4
## PRECISION AEROBATICS: MY FLIGHT TRAINING (2009-2012)

Pentagon building from the September 11th terrorist plane crash—by then, covered by an oversized American flag. His grave was flanked on all sides by identical white headstones that stretched over the hills in perfect lines as far as I could see. The ceremony was filled with tradition, a perfectly folded flag, clean uniforms, and a twenty-one-gun salute; I was sad, but also encouraged and inspired.

**That event is what I wrote about when applying for admission to the Naval Academy.** On my visits to Annapolis, I observed a similar sense of tradition, old stone buildings named after prominent Naval Officers, uniforms, and students like me, ready for a challenge. I finally received my letter and found out that I wasn't accepted. So, I went to prep school for a year and went to the Naval Academy the following year. At the time, the five-year plan seemed like a bigger deal than it is now, but it helped me realize that if I wanted to follow my dream, it wasn't going to be easy. I was going to have to work hard! And let me tell you, those four years at the Naval Academy were hard. They shaped me. I found myself in a place that constantly challenged me. And when I graduated a year ago, I had earned the title, officer, US Navy, meaning I have many more difficult challenges ahead.

**In challenging times, we rely on our faith and also the lessons we learn from the Bible to guide us.** The Bible is where we learn about the amazing life Jesus lived on earth. And His life was hard, wasn't it? He loved His enemies, He loved His neighbors as Himself, and He suffered a very painful death on the cross for us. Wow, Jesus was really tough.

**Jesus was also a leader.** Leadership was something we talked about often at the Naval Academy. Leadership can be learned and developed, but it is a true gift. Jesus had amazing personal qualities, He endured physical hardship; many people followed Him and we still do to this day; He is our model. He "talked the talk and walked the walk." Reading of His strength and how He dealt with life's challenges comforts me. Jesus learned He was called from God to live on Earth and eventually die to take away the sin of the world, to give us life. In somewhat of the same way, I've learned through reflection and prayer my calling, how the Holy

## CHAPTER 4
## PRECISION AEROBATICS: MY FLIGHT TRAINING (2009-2012)

Spirit has been working within me for some time now. I finally realized how much God truly loves us each individually. We all have been given special gifts that are meant to be shared. I try to remind myself often that it's not about me! And when I do, I feel my life becoming larger, that the possibilities are endless. God made us all different to fulfill our own purpose in life.

**To me, serving my country is my way of serving God; my way of fulfilling what I think is my calling in life.** The Oath of Office is a statement that defines my commitment [and] makes it clear that I carry out my duties with God's help. It reads as follows, "I solemnly swear that I will support and defend the Constitution of the United States against all enemies, foreign and domestic, that I will bear true faith and allegiance to the same; that I take this obligation freely, without any mental reservation or purpose of evasion; and that I will well and faithfully discharge the duties of the office upon which I am about to enter; SO HELP ME GOD."

**Just as God helps us in life today, God played a major role in the foundation of this great nation; God was invited into the inception of**

**America.** In the Declaration of Independence, Thomas Jefferson wrote that "that all men are created equal, that they are endowed by their Creator with certain inalienable rights, among these are life, liberty, and the pursuit of happiness." Independence Day celebrates the adoption of this document on July 4th, 1776, when the thirteen original colonies announced they were finally independent states. And this document proves they did this with God's help as well! The rebellious people of England came to America to be free, the way they believed God wanted us to live. This freedom allows us today to carry out our life's call in our very own unique ways. I volunteered for my job, which is a good thing because it's not for everybody. Quite frankly, women were not originally deemed qualified for military service or even designed to fit in this uniform!

**As Americans, we are blessed to be free, unlike any other nation.** Our country was founded on the principles of Christianity. There is no doubt God played a role in our becoming a free nation. In return, he simply requests our attention and devotion to Him and His principles. God wants us to be in a relationship with Him.

## CHAPTER 4
## PRECISION AEROBATICS: MY FLIGHT TRAINING (2009-2012)

We strive to comprehend the mystery of God's will. Even when I didn't understand God, He was shaping a person capable of overcoming challenges, helping me face a life I never imagined and providing the strength and skill I've needed to succeed. It's shocking to reflect on how the events in our lives happen for specific reasons; whether good or bad. God is always with us. We can invite God on our paths with us, attempting to walk with Jesus in the same direction at the same pace, even when we want to go our own way. No one said this walk would be easy! I offer that whenever we align our lives with God's path, that only good things will happen. And if more Christians in this country sought this goal, whether military servicemen and women, teachers, parents, and even politicians, don't you think our aim would be truer, more pleasing to God?

**The challenges our nation currently faces can be very discouraging.** We are fighting terrorism abroad and fighting an oil spill and a recovering economy in addition to dealing with our own personal daily struggles. My mother was diagnosed with life-threatening cancer last December. When I first received that phone call, it broke my heart. It has been a very tough time for my mother and my family. I remember immediately talking with her about the Bible story of Job and how God purposely allowed the devil to place terrible obstacles in Job's life; God really tested his faithful servant. When I was able to make the trip home to be with my mom, we read through this Bible story together. The story of Job, Jesus's life, fighting cancer, fighting a war, or any difficulty or personal hardship, solidifies the fact that real faith is refined in the fires and storms of pain. During our hard times, we sometimes ask, "Jesus, where are you?" Do we doubt that God is actually in control? He is still seated on the highest thrown [sic], He hasn't moved! We all face challenges; our nation faces challenges. We must remember that God knows us best. It is our job to listen to what it is He is telling us to do; He wants to walk with us!

**In closing, Lord, I pray for this congregation and for the celebration of our gift of independence; the gift of being American.** I believe that America and our way of life are worthy of my greatest protective effort. I ask the help of God and realize that it is only with God's help that He will make my effort great enough. Father, walk with all of us forever and always on our paths to the cross. God bless America. Amen.

## CHAPTER 4
## PRECISION AEROBATICS: MY FLIGHT TRAINING (2009-2012)

I hope you found my words clarifying as to who I was and what I stood for—but also comforting. We all have similar feelings about ourselves, our families, our friends, our higher power, be it God, Jesus, Allah, Muhammad, Buddha, etc. Yet, even at that time in my life, I was still trying to clarify who Valerie Cappelaere was all about.

Oh, yeah. I almost forgot. Now, I do not want to offend anyone as to my passionate religious beliefs. That's just who I was. If you believe in someone or something else, that's okay. If you do not believe in God, that's okay too. But, please, just believe in something. We all have a strategic place in this world. We all matter. And we all need a spiritual anchor to keep us steady and focused.

## 2011

Constantly on the move when you want to be a US Navy aviator, I was sent to NAS Meridian, Mississippi, where I flew the T-45 Goshawk. FYI: You do move around a lot when you are in the military. This in itself is not a bad thing, but you need to be aware of it if you choose this career path. PS: I highly recommend it to all!

It was here that I met the only other female student pilot in the training squadron.

My friend, Jenny Moore, described me as quite a loving and supportive friend and comrade in arms. "She and I were two of the only female flight students in Meridian, Mississippi, in 2010. We became instant friends and critical support for each other as we went through the challenges of jet fighter training together. We both needed each other and supported each other during some very difficult times, and continued to be that support for each other through the rest of our flight careers . . . You see, T-45 training in Meridian was very difficult . . . Val struggled with a new grade system, loss of confidence sometimes, questioning the whole thing and if it was worth it to continue. She failed her first carrier qualification, and that was after multiple other setbacks throughout flight training. It was discouraging. She just kept her head up and kept chugging along. She did her best on every single event, and did not give up even though some days that seemed much easier . . . Val never lost sight of her dream or why she started. She also kept reminding me during my own struggles why I started and encouraged me to keep going," said Jenny.

In my case, the friendship I found in the military was incredible. Yeah, I called her "Jenny" most of the time, but by her call sign, Clara, when trying to encourage her. "Val wrote me a card before my initial carrier qual [qualification] and the first line said, 'You are the little engine that could!' She was always so positive and encouraging. She also referenced me as 'Clara, the girl with lots of [courage],'" Jenny said.

But remember that in life, with the positive again comes the negative. To be blunt, we all have an expiration date. We just don't know it.

My precious nephew, big sister Caroline's infant son, PJ, was eulogized on Sunday, September 4, 2011. Like when mom got breast cancer back in December 2010, I knew that I had to step up and be an active warrior for spiritual matters with respect to my family and friends.

## CHAPTER 4
## PRECISION AEROBATICS: MY FLIGHT TRAINING (2009–2012)

I even sang at the funeral, as Caroline remembered. "She had the most beautiful voice. She wasn't crazy about the song we chose then either, so she also sang 'Amazing Grace.' Every time I hear either song, I think of her and it brings tears to my eyes," said Caroline.

Yep, I had to step up. Whenever I needed to best express myself, I turned to writing my thoughts and feelings on paper and then sending them in a letter to my loved ones.

Jenny Moore recalled this trait: "Val . . . was so thoughtful with me, she wrote encouraging notes, gave me a Bible, called to check up on me after a flight I was nervous about. She did that with all of her friends and family."

As did my Big Sis, Caroline, who said, "Val wrote many letters to me when my son received a terminal diagnosis, and I was struggling so hard with the fact that I would lose my first and only child at the time before he was one year old. She helped deepen my faith in God and, after my son passed away, she helped me tremendously during my grieving process."

## NOVEMBER 2011

Remember that in Summer 2007, I met my future husband, Sean Delaney, a fellow classmate at USNA, while we were training in Singapore and Australia. The funny thing is, romance was the farthest thing from my mind. Fact is, I was really struggling with carrier landings, and that was my focus. But God sometimes brings unexpected people into your life at unexpected times. The trick is, are you paying attention?

At this stage of the game, Sean and I were coming closer together. We were both sent to the *USS Ronald Reagan*, NAS North Island, San Diego. Sean qualified for carrier landings in the T-45. Even though I landed my jet several times on the carrier, I did not qualify. Anyway, I did get to spend time off the coast of California—taking off and landing on an aircraft carrier in the Pacific Ocean!

My mentor and friend, Commander Jonathan Stevenson, summed up my aircraft carrier quandary: "Her first attempt to qualify to land on an aircraft carrier didn't go well. She had to try again about a month later. She obviously learned to land, but more than that, it was 'adapt and overcome' put into practice."

I must interject here that I, Valerie Cappelaere, was not afraid to ask for help from people like Jonathan. Truth be told, that is not a sign of weakness, but a sign of strength—the element of a true leader.

"I don't think opinions mattered to her, but she was very involved in reaching out to people for mentorship as well as reaching back to provide guidance to those coming behind her," said Jonathan.

It . . . was a heady time. I gave the training my all. Mia reminded me of this trying time. "Val and I were both challenged in those first couple of years in the fleet (Navy/Marine Corps operational forces). It could be lonely, being away from your friends and family, working at something really difficult, competing with your peers. But she showed up for me in Joshua Tree (California) for one day because it was only a three-hour drive from where she was training.

## CHAPTER 4
### PRECISION AEROBATICS: MY FLIGHT TRAINING (2009–2012)

And I showed up for her—in San Diego (California) for one day because it was only a three-hour drive from where I was stationed and she was again training. I'm so grateful we did those drives, even just for one day," said Mia.

## JANUARY 2012

From here, I was sent to the *USS George H. W. Bush* at NAS Key West, Florida, and qualified for carrier landings. Alas, my training moved forward . . . and, I made it!

## FEBRUARY 2012

At the age of twenty five, I became a Navy jet pilot! Sean Delaney, by now my "wing man," and Commander Jonathan Stevenson flew to NAS Meridian, Mississippi, to pin on my Wings of Gold in February 2012!

*Naval Aviator Insignia (Image credit: Wikipedia)*

Sean and I got to fly home together for our wedding weekend, which was actually President's Day weekend. I had wallowed through the mire of the deepest valley and arduously clawed, inched, and climbed my way to the top of the greatest mountain: becoming a Navy pilot. My dream, through careful planning and a lot of hard work, was finally a reality.

## FEBRUARY 18, 2012

Sean and I were married at the US Naval Academy Chapel in Annapolis, Maryland, with a reception at the Lowes Hotel on West Street.

Before I describe the blissful matrimonial ceremony, you gotta hear the backstory. Sean and I began dating during our Youngster (sophomore) year at the Naval Academy. Sean was lucky enough to maintain the relationship throughout flight school, though he definitely tested the limits with me a time or two. Naturally, being a Navy student pilot, I was a wholly self-sufficient and independent girlfriend. While we were going through Advanced Flight Training in the T-45 at Naval Air Station Meridian, Mississippi, Sean picked out a weekend to make the proposal happen.

While I casually brought up marriage and cited not needing an engagement ring to actually get engaged, Sean started some background research. On one visit home to Maryland, he stealthily received the blessing from my mom and papa to ask for my hand in marriage.

The next step was finding the ring. Knowing I had a specific taste, Sean sought out a unique ring to surprise me. The perfect ring was found through a small jeweler, and a weekend was marked on the calendar to propose.

As fall set in on the Magnolia State, Sean planned for a camping weekend in the adjacent Cotton State. Although white tablecloths and red wine would have done the trick, he opted for the more laid-back approach that few other women would approve of as a suitable proposal site.

After setting up the campground, Sean launched into

## CHAPTER 4
## PRECISION AEROBATICS: MY FLIGHT TRAINING (2009–2012)

a dissertation, which covered the first instant when our paths crossed in Australia, through the bumpy roads we experienced (as many couples do), and into the present state of our relationship.

As Sean built up the moment, he acknowledged my earlier ingenious idea that we could be engaged without a ring, and asked what I thought about it now. Secretly, albeit momentarily crestfallen—if not a bit angry—I skeptically accepted the notion as being reasonable.

It was at this moment of skepticism that Sean got down on a knee, laughingly proposed without a ring in hand, then surprisingly slipped an engagement band onto my hand.

The proposal was initially met with shock, which quickly turned into excitement, and was finally met with approval and acceptance, to which Sean was greatly relieved. I mean, who can keep their man in that much suspense? We were officially engaged! Well, it was the wedding of all weddings!

People always wonder, is there such a thing as love at first sight? Let me tell you here and now, it does exist. It's real. When I first met Sean, I knew deep in my heart that he was absolutely the love of my life.

My good friend and fellow naval aviator, Er, noted this as well: "When they first met, I whispered to Val, 'He's wonderful . . . Go get him!' She [meaning me, Val] responded, without missing a beat, 'I'm planning on it,'" said Erin Rawlick Delaney.

And so, on Saturday, February 18, 2012, I wed my best friend, USNA classmate, and comrade in arms, Sean Delaney, at the Naval Academy Chapel in Annapolis, Maryland, just days after earning my pilot wings!

Yep, I didn't miss a beat. Though we had our "ups and downs" like all couples do, we decided to "adapt and overcome"—to dive for success, to take that challenge on.

My mom helped me tremendously. "I loved planning Val's wedding with her in late 2011. She was in flight school, so a lot of it had to be done remotely. She came home at Thanksgiving to try on gowns and again at Christmas for fittings...Val and Sean had the most beautiful fairy tale wedding at the Naval Academy Chapel," she said.

I'm telling you, the struggle was worth it. As fate would have it, I was then assigned to NAS Whidbey Island in Washington state, about twenty-five miles north of Seattle in the Puget Sound. This was my dream assignment! Let me tell you, this place was so beautiful, a serendipitous sign of things to come. Life seemed so perfect, yet the Navy waits for no one. I received orders to report to NAS Whidbey Island, Washington, to train to fly the EA-6B Prowler.

"Val's first assignment was to VAQ129 in Whidbey Island, Washington, where she trained to fly the EA-6B Prowler for the Navy. She moved out there from Meridian, Mississippi, after she was married. Sean was already out there, so I got to drive cross country with her. We took about a week, and she had planned the route. It was an amazing trip and time with her," said Doreen Cappelaere.

## SPRING/SUMMER 2012

As my naval career was taking flight, so, too, was my life with Sean. We built a house in Anacortes, Washington. Together, living the dream. All of our stars had aligned.

## CHAPTER 4
### PRECISION AEROBATICS: MY FLIGHT TRAINING (2009-2012)

Sean really appreciated me for me, and I for him. We will eternally treasure that friendship bond of deep love and admiration. We understood each other.

"Valerie worked hard at everything she did, including trying to be the best wife she could be. Although known for being incredibly beautiful, smart, athletic, fun, and outgoing, it was her unyielding compassion and excitement for life that I fell in love with most. From hunting and hiking . . . to wine tasting and fine dining, she was one I could do anything with. Simply put, she was my best friend," said Sean.

**WINGS FOR VAL:** MEMOIR OF A YOUNG FEMALE PILOT

Chapter 5

# LOW-LEVEL MISSION: CHECK SIX (2013)

---

I am excited today. Today is my second attempt to fly a very complicated training maneuver, and I can't wait to get at it.

... I kiss Sean, roll out of bed, get dressed in my military flight suit, and head to the kitchen.

Flight days are early. Some would say "Oh-dark-thirty" early. First there is a pre-flight briefing. Crew are introduced to each other and the mission is discussed. Pilots are experts at this, even if we have never met before, so there will be a bit of banter mixed in with our seriousness at the beginning.

Some of our preflight is done the night before, but we still need to double-check the weather, temperature, wind velocity, and direction, for example. We have math calculations to complete for weight and fuel, the course, and complete a mental practice run to clarify any uncertainties. Oh, lots to do....

And, like I said, I'm eager to get to it. So, I pour my coffee to-go and grab my keys to the car.

"I love you, Sean! See you after my flight!"

Sean pulls me in for a quick hug and a "Go get 'em, 'Mom'!"

We pause for a flash prayer, another quick kiss, and I am out the door.

My crew and I have prepared well, and the weather is cooperating. After our briefing, we grab our gear and head out to the aircraft. I do the pre-flight visual walk-around, check the fuel, oil, and pull the wheel chocks. All appears good. My bird is ready for the skies.

"It's a go!" There will be two birds flying today's mission. I will be following the calls of the echelon (aka lead plane) today.

In the Northrop Grumman EA-6B Prowler, I have the left front seat, which is the location known as "pilot in command." My instructor, Lieutenant Commander Alan A. Patterson, will be to my right, ready to help if I need it.

Behind me is Lieutenant William B. McIlvaine III. This is our first official flight together, which is pretty standard. Rotating the human element of a flight crew forces pilots to really know their aircraft and not to cover or take chances or cut corners for friends.

## CHAPTER 5
### LOW-LEVEL MISSION: CHECK SIX (2013)

The standards are elevated in this way, too. Pilots need to know their stuff. Procedures are standardized, so pilots are interchangeable with each other. Pilots all talk the same language, perform the same tasks, and fly by these set rules and regulations, the standards mandate. The rules are unwaivable, as the checklists are "written in blood," as they say. Thus, all regulations are to keep the next pilots and aircraft safe. Mistakes teach us what not to do the next time. We are always learning.

One thing you should know is that pilots must verbally state what actions they are taking. Thus, verbal communication is synonymous with action. There is no guessing or wondering what the person next to you is doing. The checklist is done in order, a verbal statement is stated as the action is being performed, and then the other person in the cockpit regurgitates it back to register the understanding.

For today's training mission, I am in a tandem flight. Military pilots fly in formation for safety. Think mutual defense with safety in numbers, with a concentration of firepower, should trouble arise. If you have seen the movie, *Top Gun* (1986), you get an idea why Navy flying in tandem is a good tactic to take. Thus, learning tactical maneuvers is an important part of flight training. Sure, there is a danger to having two planes so close to each other in the air, but it is a necessary risk.

This is a good challenge for me. Do you have good challenges? You know, those difficult tasks that are hard but worth doing . . . like Math class or Physics?

Well, I'm clear for takeoff, so I turn on to the active

runway. I am at the right of the echelon. That makes me his wingman for this exercise. For takeoff, we do not have to use the radio. We have standard hand and head signals, and we treat the centerline like it is a brick wall. That mental picture of a brick wall keeps us where we both need to be while on the runway.

Takeoff is a joy to me, but I am all business—nailing some new maneuvers today. Ever hear of muscle memory? Time to get some, and I am up to the task.

I push the throttle forward, the engines roar to life, and we accelerate down the runway and lift off! I stow the landing gear and I continue to pre-set low-level training route and set altitude. The skies are freeing! And it's a go:

> I bank right.
> Check.
> Above the hard deck.
> Check.
> I bank left.
> Check.
> Above the hard deck.
> Check.
> Recover.
> The next maneuver is a practiced walk in the park. Here we go!
> Ninety-degree turn . . . and I'm still with my echelon.
> Check.
> Reverse turn, flip, bleep.
> My lead is calling for me.
> My plane is silent.
> I cannot return to base.

# CHAPTER 5
## LOW-LEVEL MISSION: CHECK SIX (2013)

For some reason the jet I was piloting swirled down uncontrollably from the sky and crashed into a nearby farm field. I can tell you with absolute certainty that the malfunction happened so quickly that the three of us onboard were not able to react or eject.

We didn't have our recovery needs.

What do I mean by that?

There are three piloting priorities during a flight emergency: aviate, navigate, and communicate. I needed altitude to use all three of those tools. However, on a low-level training mission, altitude is in short supply and thus all three of the necessary recovery needs were not available.

What happened?

On Monday, March 11, 2013, I perished in a flight accident near Spokane in eastern Washington state during a training mission while flying a Grumman EA-6B Prowler for (Electronic Attack Squadron) VAQ 129, headquartered at NAS Whidbey Island, Washington state.

What went wrong? I might or might not know; it happened in a blink of an eye. For me and the crew, the what, why, and how no longer matter. There was absolutely no indication that things would go wrong that day.

My mom even noted this. "Val would call us almost every day . . . We knew from flight to flight whether it was good or bad," Doreen said on ABC 7 News. It was clear skies, good weather, and a talented crew.

Several people witnessed both the flying of the plane and the resulting fatal crash.

"Karen Carlson . . . said she was talking on the phone

when she heard what she thought was a sonic boom; Mike Johnson . . . saw a black mushroom cloud. And Larry Zagelow said . . . 'I've never seen anything like that,'" according to news reports on Spokesman.com.

Death is never easy to accept for anyone who is loved by someone or for another person you've loved.

Oh, like my mom and papa ...

Back in Maryland, it was an ordinary spring day. Nothing unusual. As part of my mom's fight to win against cancer, she needed to take better care of herself. So, about the time I was lifting off the ground, she was walking down the street to join her yoga class at a neighbor's home.

Thus, my mom was not at home when the home phone rang. As fate would have it, Papa answered: "Hi, Sean." It was my husband on the other end.

"Hi, Patrice," he said in a very unsteady voice.

Alarmed by Sean's voice, Papa questioned, "What's wrong, Sean?"

"There's been an accident. It's Val. Her jet went down..."

My beloved Sean was trying to convey the information through his own shock and grief. Details such as "Val was flying an EA-6B Prowler in clear skies from Whidbey Island Naval Air Station heading over the mountains toward Spokane, Washington" were difficult to register with my papa.

But somewhere in there, papa understood that "Val was part of a two-plane training mission. She was flying in the left front seat as pilot in command . . . The plane went down . . . Patrice, there are no survivors . . ."

This was news no husband or parent or loved one

## CHAPTER 5
### LOW-LEVEL MISSION: CHECK SIX (2013)

ever wants to hear. My husband and my father had another immediate burden to bear.

Mom was at yoga.

My mom bravely recalled: "It wasn't long until Patrice showed up to my yoga class, which he had never done before. I noticed him but didn't think much of it. He talked to the instructor for a few moments and then they came and got me out of class.

"They told me what had happened to Val's flight. I wasn't sure exactly what they were saying. I was in shock. This *cannot* be true. Patrice held me. As we exited the house to head home, something finally hit my brain. Not Val..."

"NOOOOOO!" Mom shouted!

At a loss for words, my mom screamed in anguish, "AHHHHH!" She screamed again. And she screamed again, and again! Neighbors started coming outside. Her yoga buddies were concerned. "AHHHHHH!" The words closed in.

The entire block of their neighborhood knew something was terribly wrong. First the loss of their infant grandson, PJ, and now Val. "I need my girls!"

How can anyone forget this pain? Will it ever subside?

So, are you still asking what really happened? The Navy sent out a lot of experts within hours of the crash to try and figure it out. It's interesting to note that this plane, the EA-6B Prowler, which is used for jamming enemy radar systems, dates back to at least 1971. It was removed from service in June of 2015, two years after my crash, according to PeriscopeFilm.

We three Navy pilots, McIlvaine III, Patterson, and me, were not the only ones to have crashed in this type of plane. As was noted at the time of the tragedy on March 11, 2013, "In eastern Oregon, a Prowler crashed in 2006, but the crew safely ejected, and in 2001 another crashed on the Olympic Peninsula in western Washington, according to news reports . . . It's the same type of warplane that was being flown by a Marine crew in 1998 during a low-altitude flight when it clipped a gondola cable in Italy, killing twenty civilians," according to Spokesman.com.

I was the last of two Navy student pilots to train in this aircraft, the EA-6B Prowler. The base and squadron command lost focus of the training mission due to various factors: I was asked to fly this very difficult, complex, and dangerous mission when—in hindsight—I was not prepared properly for the mission. My instructor, even though technically qualified, lacked the hours required to safely monitor the low-level maneuvers I was attempting. In the final analysis, it's as if the US Navy command failed *its mission*.

Ironically, one of my instructors had recently told me that I was doing great. My mom recalls: "The instructor had told her that she [me, Valerie Cappelaere Delaney!] was one of the best students that he had flown with in a long time," as reported by Linda So for WMAR-2 News.

I'm speechless at this point. Let me say that it really hurts to think that this could have even happened. You know me by now! I always took my training so seriously. Furthermore, my CO of the Electronic Attack Squadron VAQ 129, Commander Chris Middleton, noted how "she loved to fly . . . She was

## CHAPTER 5
### LOW-LEVEL MISSION: CHECK SIX (2013)

simply an inspiration to all that knew her," Chris said on WhidbeyNewsTimes.com.

Success is not easy. You surely know that by now through my life's struggles delineated in this book you are now reading.

Now, this is so important... Don't feel sorry for me. *Learn from me.* Death is a part of life. In fact, death is an aerial mission that we all must fly. Some . . . simply land before the others. But we all end up on the same runway in the end, don't we?

Yes, the more I think of this truly human notion, the more I realize that my last flight is really a metaphor for life. We all take off and soar, some high, some not so high . . . and some land softly and some land hard. But *we all land eventually.* The point is we challenge ourselves—despite the odds or expectations or dangers—to fly.

I challenged myself, and you can challenge yourself too. You may say, "Life is not fair, Val. Your life was easy compared to mine." To which I, Valerie Cappelaere Delaney, must agree. I was blessed with a loving nuclear and extended family who did not horribly mistreat me.

Some of you may read my book and think simply, "Val has no idea how I feel. She could never be successful if she had lived my life." To that, I answer, "You're right. I have not lived your life. In fact, I cannot hold a candle to you. But I have died young and you are still alive. That's the trade-off. We are equal through our respective loss: You lost love but have your life; I had love but lost my life.

*So, why don't you let my life be your lesson?*

Never fear death. Honor life. Honor God and your legacy to the world. It's not when or how you die but how you live that matters. As Selena Quintanilla, the "Queen of Tejano Music," stated, "The goal isn't to live forever but to create something that will."

You see, when it's all said and done, can you say with certainty that you lived your life to the fullest? Without fear? Without prejudice? Without . . . limitations imposed upon yourself or by others?

Put another way, Chicano musician and historian Mark Guerrero stated that life is indubitably short, and that you should "enjoy the ride living in the moment . . . [while] valuing your relationships and being kind to others. We're all in the same boat." Have you lived your life like this?

So, please. Do me the honor. Live your life to the fullest. Don't hold back. Fear not. Dent that universe. Don't let mistakes stop you. Your destiny awaits you. Dream. Plan. Act. And in due time, we will meet on another plane.

Anyway, here, at this point in my story, I must bid you a very heartfelt and joyful "Adieu!" Others must now continue to live by my example, to tell my story. Will you?

May God Bless you and your loved ones always!

It's "Mom" signing out.

# VAL'S PHOTO GALLERY

All photos are courtesy of the Cappelaere family unless otherwise noted.

*Me, Rex, Allison, and Caroline at our home in Ellicott City, Maryland.*

*Me with my best buddy, Rex.*

## VAL'S PHOTO GALLERY

*My family; Valerie, Patrice, Doreen, Caroline, and Allison.*

*Caroline and me (age twelve) at a wedding in France.*

*Ready for battle; My official high school lacrosse photo.*

*Sports changed me; My freshman year soccer photo.*

VAL'S PHOTO GALLERY

*Hard work pays off. Here I am at age eighteen.*

*Here I am with Congressman Elijah Cummings.
(Photo courtesy of Patrice Cappelaere.)*

*I Day with Papa and an old cell phone.*

*This is me on I Day with my sisters, Caroline and Allison.*

VAL'S PHOTO GALLERY

*Here I am participating in PEP.*

*Here I am front and center with my company during Plebe Summer.*

*Here I am in the middle with my sister, Allison, and my mom, Doreen, at a boxing smoker at the academy.*

*One Halloween at the academy, I dressed as Marilyn Monroe and Erin as a Ninja Turtle.*

VAL'S PHOTO GALLERY

*"Esprit de corps!"*
*(Photo courtesy of Patrice Cappelaere.)*

*Here I am with Allison at the Grand Canyon in Arizona.*
*(Photo courtesy of Allison Righter.)*

*Commander Jonathan Stevenson and me on the day of my first ride in an F-18. (Photo courtesy of Jonathan Stevenson.)*

*Day of my first ride in an F-18. (Photo courtesy of Jonathan Stevenson.)*

## VAL'S PHOTO GALLERY

*I'm pictured here in Paris with two of my very tall Saint Cyr Military Academy classmates.*

*Leading the troops!*
*(Photo courtesy of Patrice Cappelaere.)*

*I completed the Marine Corps Marathon!*

*I was able to attend Caroline's wedding.*
*(Photo credit: Kristin and Bruce Castenschiold Photography.)*

VAL'S PHOTO GALLERY

*I accepted my diploma from the Commander in Chief and 44th President of the United States, Barack Obama. (Photo courtesy of Patrice Cappelaere.)*

*My smile says it all! I earned my diploma.
(Photo courtesy of Patrice Cappelaere.)*

Rite of Passage: I receive my first salute as an officer from my friend, Mia Stender. (Photo courtesy of Patrice Cappelaere.)

*Standing on the wing of a T-34 Turbo Mentor.
(Photo credit: Pete Lutz f/6.3 Studio.)*

*I am in the front seat of this T-45 Goshawk.*

*At my winging ceremony with Sean Delaney (left) and Jon Stevenson (right).*

VAL'S PHOTO GALLERY

*Mr. and Mrs. Delaney.*
*(Photo credit: Kristin and Bruce Castenschiold Photography.)*

*My wedding day; pure joy!*
*(Photo credit: Kristin and Bruce Castenschiold Photography.)*

*Solid as an oak tree.*
*(Photo credit: Kristin and Bruce Castenschiold Photography.)*

*With Sean when I arrived in Washington state.*

# VAL'S PHOTO GALLERY

*One of my flight suit patches.*

*"Mom" getting ready to take off.*

*Leaning against a T-34 Turbo Mentor. (Photo credit: Pete Lutz f/6.3 Studio.)*

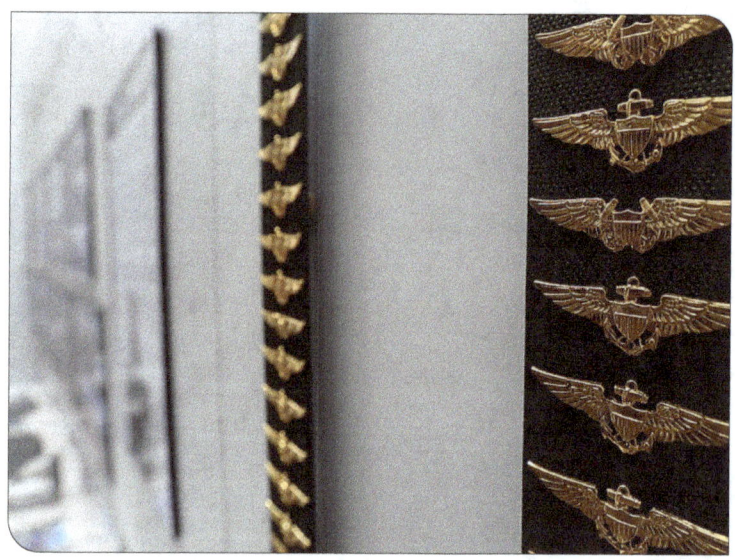

*A closeup of the "Wings for Val" at the Women's Memorial at Arlington National Cemetery. (Photo Credit: Jess Atkinson)*

# Part 2
# VAL'S LEGACY
---

# Chapter 6

# DEBRIEF: ADAPT AND OVERCOME

---

Lieutenant Valerie Cappelaere Delaney passed away that day. We who loved her needed to debrief this tragic loss: What did Val mean to each of us? We needed to grieve. We did this not only by talking about the sadness of her passing, but also the joy of her life—and how Val personally touched our lives. The following quotes are just a sampling of Val's powerful and inspirational significance.

**Deborah Bandy wrote in *Aero Crew News:*** "When anyone dies, regardless of the circumstances, those left behind look for meaning, the legacy of that life . . . Albeit brief, Val's life touched so many in countless positive ways."

*There was a memorial service held for Val and her crew members where they were stationed at NAS Whidbey Island on Tuesday, March 19, 2013.*

"Well over 1,200 family members, friends, guests from the local and base communities, and other dignitaries joined VAQ 129 at a memorial service . . . for Lieutenant Commander Alan A. Patterson, Lieutenant Junior Grade Valerie C. Delaney, and Lieutenant Junior Grade William McIlvaine III," according to WhidbeyNewsTimes.com.

*There was also a memorial service for Val at her family's church, Saint John's Episcopal Church in Ellicott City, Maryland on Saturday, May 18, 2013.*

**Val's father, Patrice Cappelaere,** gave heartfelt commentary about his daughter's life:

"This is not a eulogy.

This is not even the speech I had written a few weeks ago. I kept hearing a little voice in the back of my head saying: 'Throw that away, this is not what I want to say.' So I had to throw it away and start over. So here is what Val wants to say...

"It's not about how to achieve your dreams. It's about how to lead your life. If you lead your life the right way, the karma will take care of itself. The dreams will come to you...

"Appreciate the miracle of being alive, accept failures, your own imperfections, and become the person God wants you to be.

"There is much we need to be grateful for. It is only with struggles and the help of angels that we can achieve things far beyond our own capabilities. With so much gratitude, I have never forgotten my friends and kept helping others. Now an angel myself, I will help you.

"I will share that secret with you, my friend. A secret I discovered during my own journey and sometimes the hard way.

"Know what you want and do not waste time.

## CHAPTER 6
### DEBRIEF: ADAPT AND OVERCOME

"Challenges are there to be met or to make us stronger and learn. Believe in yourself. You are not perfect, but worthy of love; I love you and God loves you. I want to see that gleam in your eyes and a smile on your face as I had in mine. Talk to your heart. Talk to my heart and one day, you will hear the voice.

"[Success] . . . does not come easily...

"Accept my help and God's help. And it will be granted. This is my first step. You need heart and faith. It takes work. Get on it.

"You will also need your body. And that takes more work. So, start training every day, rain or shine...

"Of course, you will have to work your brain hard as well, but that's the easiest task. It may not feel like work, as it is your destiny to become you.

"Carry with you at all times these three things: faith, hope, and love. Nothing will stop you. You will have no fear. Then it will be your turn to help and encourage the little ones around you...

"Saint-Exupéry, a French aviator, told us another secret in the Little Prince: 'It is very simple: It is only with the heart that one can see.' True. You may not see me, but I am here.

"The Little Prince continues: 'You will have stars as no one else has them... In one of the stars, I shall be living. In one of them, I shall be laughing. When you look at the sky at night . . . You—only you—will find me! This is my present. And when your sorrow is comforted (time soothes all sorrows) you will be content that you have known me...'

"Remember, I am not that far away, I'm just in your heart,

invisible to your eyes, but I'm there. You will always find me when you need me."

*Various family members and friends joined publicly or through statements (read by family friend Daria Malan) in remembering Val, her life, her impact on her family, her friends, her community.*

**Cappelaere family friend, Daria Malan:** "Valerie was such an impressive person, it seemed difficult for me to express myself in a way that would justly describe who she was to all of us."

**Val's younger sister, Allison Righter:** "Valerie was my friend and mentor . . . The rock of our family . . . hard-headed, feisty and fearless . . . the most stylish with the best and most expensive taste . . . She was funny . . . maybe couldn't take a joke . . . yet totally not afraid to make a fool of herself . . . Selective with her friends and who she chose to surround herself with . . ."

**Val's grandmother, Carolyn Drake:** "Valerie loved to sing! She was a member of the Glee Club at the Naval Academy and a member of the coveted acapella group, The Stowaways. Val sang at Caroline's wedding . . . And with all her heart, she sang in the hardest of situations: At her nephew, PJ's, funeral . . . Val's beautiful voice is now resounding from heaven."

**Val's high school guidance counselor, Jenn McKnight:** "She was gifted in math and science . . . Val KNEW where she was going and built a solid foundation for a degree in Engineering and possessed the academic ability required for success at the Naval Academy . . . Perhaps the

## CHAPTER 6
### DEBRIEF: ADAPT AND OVERCOME

quality I admired most about Valerie was her INTEGRITY. Although outstanding in so many areas, Valerie was also a down-to-earth, typical teenager . . . Valerie did not escape high school without experiencing one such life lesson. When confronted with the situation Valerie owned up to her mistake, accepted her consequence, and then she came to see me because she was driven to influence other students to avoid similar mistakes."

**Daria Malan:** "As a hospital administrator, I had the opportunity to have all three Cappelaere girls spend their summers with me for their high school community service hours . . . As you can imagine, they were exposed to situations that they had never seen before. It was a growth opportunity for them. But Valerie turned her experience into a growth opportunity for the patients and staff. The patients on the Stroke Unit were quite impaired, and the average age of [each] was seventy-nine. After spending just her first few days with the speech therapists, Val introduced the idea of getting the patients on the internet as part of their medical treatment plan . . . Next thing I know, these patients are on a laptop, searching the web as part of their therapy sessions. Val is sitting next to them . . . showing them what to click . . . what to read. She was just sixteen years old . . . The physicians thought she was amazing."

**Val's older sister, Caroline Desroches:** "Val treated me better than I deserve. I put her through hell growing up. I was a mean and bossy older sister, and it wasn't until I moved to college that I really started to appreciate her for the beautiful and amazing person she was . . . My biggest regret is that I don't think I told her enough . . . how much I really loved her . . . how proud of her I am . . . She never ceased to amaze me with her many talents. Not only did she pursue her dream of becoming a jet pilot, but she also learned to quilt, hunt, train for triathlons, and design/build her dream home while doing it. She never stopped . . . Val was always my strength and support growing up. Being the older sister, that probably should have been my role . . . but I was always scared and Val was always brave. Val was the strongest shoulder I had to lean on when PJ passed away. Valerie said 'Don't be so upset. PJ wouldn't want you to be. You know he's smiling down on you from heaven.' I'm comforted now because I know she's up there too."

**Val's best friend at the Naval Academy, Erin Rawlick Delaney:** "To put it simply, she was the best friend I could have ever asked for . . . I miss her every single day. She was the first upperclassman to approach me. Throughout my freshman year at the academy, Val was my rock . . . She inspired me to be a pilot; she taught me how to be a better friend. She taught me to NEVER settle and to be fearless in everything that I did."

**Daria Malan:** "I think we can agree Valerie Cappelaere Delaney was a treasure. She was gifted with uncommon determination, strength, and grit. But underneath that strength and determination is what truly set Valerie apart. She had an incredibly big heart and strong faith. In her quest to achieve her goals, she didn't climb over or push others down to rise above. Rather . . . she instinctively saw the importance of helping others and bringing them along

## CHAPTER 6
### DEBRIEF: ADAPT AND OVERCOME

WITH her . . . Hopefully, we will find some way to have the strength and support to get through this LONG PROCESS OF HEALING. And when the time is right, and we are able, we will remember the example that Valerie set and allow it to inspire us to be a LITTLE stronger, a LITTLE more determined, and A LOT kinder to everyone . . . BUT REMEMBER, Valerie left us doing WHAT SHE LOVED TO DO. So, we must TRY to heal. And we are so fortunate to have the best advice from Valerie HERSELF, who is saying to all of us today: 'ADAPT and OVERCOME.'"

---

*Yes, Lieutenant Valerie Cappelaere Delaney is gone physically, but not spiritually. That's a person's legacy. Val's legacy is a patchwork quilt sewn with an emotional chain, the strongest link being love.*

**Jonathan Stevenson:** "Val represented the ideal of who I wanted my daughters to become. I was a mentor to Val, took her on her first flight in a tactical Navy aircraft (FA-18) and had the privilege to pin on her Wings of Gold when she finished Navy flight school."

**Caroline Desroches:** "I was Val's older sister, and I think she looked up to me. We had a very close relationship, because we did so much growing up together. But even as adults when we would move away or travel, we would always make an effort to visit each other."

**John Craighill:** "I would say Val did achieve the respect of others and was respected by all who knew her."

*Being touched by grace as she was, you could feel it.*

*Others could as well and would wonder who she was. Val was beautiful inside and outside. Like the proverbial "white light in the room," Valerie Cappelaere Delaney was more than a living, breathing human being; rather, she was a strong, spiritual force of nature, who made an impact beyond the flesh and bone, pervading all with whom she encountered, touched, and embraced.*

**Caroline Desroches:** "Val wanted to be viewed as the strong, tough, beautiful woman that she was. As an adult . . . outside opinions were not important."

**Allison Righter:** "I do think Val had a tough exterior, but inside she did care about what others thought [in the beginning]. She got teased a lot growing up for being overweight and wearing glasses, so I do think she cared about her appearance and fitting in. She was naturally beautiful and also had a great taste in clothes and fashion . . . And then when it came to attending USNA and becoming a pilot, it was all about her performance and proving herself. I think she wanted to be viewed as a hardworking, relentless and competent student and eventual pilot who also cared deeply [about] people."

*Val did not fear what others thought of her. If anything, she only feared what she thought of herself; to always do the right thing for herself and others. Papa understood this as much as anyone.*

**Patrice Cappelaere:** "Val always wanted to help her teammates. She had profound impact on many of her friends."

*Val did not fear the emotional, psychological, spiritual, and physical shortcomings others might have perceived*

# CHAPTER 6
## DEBRIEF: ADAPT AND OVERCOME

*her as having, rather—and this is critical to anyone seeking solace in their own skin, their own mind, body, and spirit—she simply feared always doing herself and the people around her . . . any less than loving justice.*

**Doreen Cappelaere:** "Val had very high standards for herself and for the people she chose to be her friends. She was kind and compassionate to almost everyone."

**Erin Rawlick Delaney:** "Val considered her relationships with her family and friends to be her greatest blessings. She always prioritized the people she loved and made time to make them feel special."

**Jonathan Stevenson:** "She drew people into her sphere and made us all better people for knowing her."

*Val had a few skeletal remains in her past. But that's okay.*

**Mia Stender:** "Strong. Complex. Kind. Val felt deeply. She knew who she was. There were many challenges for her. As intelligent, poised, beautiful, compassionate, and talented as Val was—I can think of many chapters of her life that weren't what she wanted them to be, that she had to overcome."

The struggle for equal treatment of women, Val's struggle—under the law and in practice, de jure and de facto . . . continues to this day. In fact, the US women's soccer team decided to sue its boss, the US Soccer Federation, for gender discrimination on March 8, 2019. The female soccer players claim they receive worse wages, endure worse working conditions, and less media coverage than their male counterparts, according to a *Washington Post* report.

Without a doubt, Val's sacrifice as a female military aviator indirectly laid the groundwork for the sacrifice of these athletes. They are all interconnected. Women sticking together like a common propulsion system rocketing forward toward the betterment of not just women, but all mankind, that's the downhome, true biz answer to a better future for all; sacrifice equals results.

**Erin Rawlick Delaney:** "We had many conversations about the struggles of being a woman at USNA and then in flight school, especially the jet pipeline . . . Val always had to work extra hard to prove herself."

*Yes, Val has quite the legacy!*

**Caroline Desroches:** "Val LOVED being a pilot. It was a dream come true for her. I think if she was still alive and given the chance to be a mother and a pilot, it would have made her life complete . . ."

**Doreen Cappelaere:** "Becoming a Navy pilot and earning your Wings of Gold is a huge deal and the culmination of years of training and work. Val was very proud of this accomplishment. There are not many women who become military jet pilots."

*Many people believe that death is just an arbitrary state of mind, but not the reality within the realm of the belief in a spiritual world—Val's world. Doreen notes full well that Val still "visits her" and bequeaths her worldly gifts.*

**Doreen Cappelaere:** "Val was a great and loving daughter, and our love for each other will never end. She leaves me feathers at very opportune times. If I'm feeling down, I might find a beautiful feather in my garden or on the path [upon which] I walk in the woods. I have a whole collection of feathers from her; hundreds of them!"

## CHAPTER 6
### DEBRIEF: ADAPT AND OVERCOME

**"A Haiku for Val"**

*By Jim Hoffmann*

The Hand of Lord God
Broke through the quaint clouds that day
And whisked Sweet Val 'way

**"A Sonnet for Val"**

*By Jim Hoffmann*

Not in a manger, yet born in this place
Spring flowers bloomed - Valerie's epic fate
Doreen and Patrice and two sisters—grace
Young Val stood tall, ov' all, she doth equate

"She's always been fearless," said friendly face
Piloting that Prowler—a trying trait
McIlvaine, Patterson, the crew sought space
Fate betwixt tragedy - aer'al conflate

Many mourned that day of stormy embrace
Thursday, June, presidential real estate
"Almighty God, our warriors, our face
Fought for the republic, humanity's sake

Valerie, a pilot, leader so true
Said, "I know you guys will carry me through."

### "As Free as Valerie"
*By Jim Hoffmann*

**V**al's always been fearless
**A**viator— "died doing what she loved"
**L**ieutenant JG, yet twenty-six and young
**E**very heart with wings flutter
**R**emembering her sacrifice "in aeternum"
**I**n spirituality, perseverance, love
**E**veryone, everywhere, "as free as Valerie"

## Chapter 7

# WINGS TAKE FLIGHT: HOW DOES VAL INSPIRE YOU?

---

The legacy of Valerie Cappelaere Delaney began the night before her burial, Thursday, June 6, 2013. Three of Val's close friends presented the family with two seven-foot-long jump straps pinned with nearly 200 sets of aviator wings.

"We knew that Valerie was going to be buried at Arlington [National Cemetery], and I [Lieutenant Danielle Thiriot] was planning on attending the funeral service. And a few of my friends who had been Valerie's teammates in college, and who had known her in flight school, were unable to attend. And I said, 'I'm going to take my wings off and leave them at Arlington with her.' And, another one of the ladies said, 'You know, I can't come. Could you please take my wings too?' So, we had two sets of wings. And she said, 'Would you mind if I emailed a couple of my teammates who are in Whidbey Island, to bring their wings as well?' I said, 'Sure! Give them my address.' And the response was . . . overwhelming."

What started out as a small gesture of friends who couldn't be there—but who offered their hard-earned pilot wings in love, support, and solidarity—snowballed into wings from female aviators from all over the world and all branches of the service.

The funeral service included full military honors and even a missing man flyover of four F-18's (jets) from NAS Oceana, Virginia. In attendance were her family, friends, and military personnel spanning up and down the ranks.

"The true testament of her impact on others could be visibly seen on a nearby table where over 200 gold and silver aviator wings were on display. These small uniform badges represent the enormous effort and sacrifice necessary to successfully complete the rigorous training required to become a military aviator. All the wings had been earned and worn by women in the military aviation community and sent—from all over the world—to honor Valerie's life. Some had engravings on the back from loved ones, and some even came from the Air Force and other different branches of the military. Many were from people who knew Valerie. Yet others were from strangers who understood and truly felt the bond among women in aviation," said Courtney Vandament, one of Val's former plebes.

When fellow female aviators presented the wings to Valerie's parents, they said: "There are not many women in military aviation. As the youngest generation of junior officers, we understand our success depends on the support we give each other. To be successful as a minority we must not only reach forward to seek mentorship but also reach back to

# CHAPTER 7
## WINGS TAKE FLIGHT: HOW DOES VAL INSPIRE YOU?

support and inspire those behind us. 'Mom' (Valerie's call sign) understood this better than anyone and was a source of strength to girls both older and younger. Individually, these wings represent amazing personal accomplishment. Together, they celebrate the strength we give each other and the collective strength of all female aviators," said Danielle Thiriot.

This is how Val's family got the idea to start the foundation and to carry on her incredible legacy. The various female pilots wrote in a letter, "We leave our wings with Val and take her with us as we fly," said Danielle.

As the old adage goes, "All gave some. Some gave all." Lieutenant Valerie Cappelaere Delaney was laid to rest at Arlington National Cemetery. She died protecting our freedom . . . the ultimate sacrifice.

"Valerie Cappelaere Delaney was promoted posthumously to Lieutenant and awarded the Navy Achievement Medal for her dedication and passion for the aviation community and her service to the nation," wrote Courtney Vandament.

## "HOW DOES VAL INSPIRE YOU?"

So . . . What does Lieutenant Valerie Cappelaere Delaney's story mean to you? Are YOU ready to take action?

Craft a response to any of the prompts below and email the response (in picture form if necessary) to:

**info@wingsforval.org**

Or mail it to:
**Wings for Val Foundation**
**7680 Colonial Beach Road**
**Pasadena, Maryland, 21122**

- **Prompt 1:** Discuss or write a brief message of Val's legacy.
- **Prompt 2:** Create a brief poem, or song lyric worthy of Val's legacy.
- **Prompt 3:** Draw a picture worthy of Val's legacy.
- **Prompt 4:** Consider your dreams for your life: Write them down.
- **Prompt 5:** What is your plan to achieve those dreams? Write it down.

Yes, "adapt and overcome" was Val's motto. *Now these words are your words.* What will you do with them? Are you ready to take your dreams all the way? Do you see that the sky is not the limit, but the beginning? Are you ready to "adapt and overcome?" Like Val, let nothing stop you.

# AFTERWORD

As I walked the halls of the Women in Aviation Conference as a junior in college, I found myself among incredible women including air traffic controllers, aviation managers, airport directors, pilots, and military aviators. I started to let myself dream. Though I had always admired the women who don the uniform and serve our country, I never let myself believe I could be one of them, especially as a military aviator. They were in the same category of superheroes to me.

It was then I found myself at the Wings for Val booth. I was immediately intrigued and welcomed by Doreen's warm smile as she started to tell me about her daughter. I was enraptured and listened intently. In Lieutenant Cappelaere Delaney's path, I saw myself. The similarities abounded. When Doreen asked me about my life and goals, I told her something that no one else knew. I had an "impossible" dream of becoming a US Air Force pilot. A dream I had barely admitted to myself. I told her of my life, my successes, challenges, and my desire to serve honorably. "You are just like her," she said, "don't let the fear of the unknown stop you." Those words impacted me tenfold. Taking Doreen's words of encouragement and embracing Lieutenant Cappelaere Delaney's spirit, I applied to the USAF to become an officer.

I had just finished my master's degree, in the middle of the USAF application process, and was working in Washington, DC, when Val became more than just an inspiration. One weekend, I headed to Arlington National

Cemetery. Arlington—already hallowed grounds as the final resting place for those who gave the ultimate sacrifice—became more meaningful to me that day. As I walked the halls of the Women in Military Service for America Memorial, I saw the display case dedicated to Lieutenant Cappelaere Delaney. I cried reading the dedication and my heart swelled at the meaning behind the rows of aviator wings that adorned the wall. I then visited the memorial to her and her crew located in Arlington. I left a nickel, an aviation tradition, to her and her crew, took a moment of silence in their memory, and sent a prayer of love to their families.

On my return to the front gates, I discovered her resting place. The woman who had inspired me to live my dreams transformed in a moment from a story, a spirit, and an entity, to corporeal and real. I sat there under the shade of a tree at the foot of her grave . . . for hours. I returned time and time again to talk, visit, and update her on my progress. Lieutenant Cappelaere Delaney became Val to me in those months, and when I left, it was like leaving a friend.

Then the Air Force called me back with a decision. I knew I had an angel over my shoulder as I was notified that I was selected to realize my dream—to become an officer in the World's Greatest Air Force—and to serve as a pilot!

Every day I wear a black bracelet in her memory. It has three lines. The first line has her name and the rank she earned. The second line has her birthdate, the date that she was celebrated into this world, and a dash. That all-so-important dash, the smallest symbol—is also the most meaningful. That dash holds the life that she filled to the fullest by living her dreams, loving fiercely, and fighting for her people. It also has her death date, the date she left this world but also transcended her roles as a daughter, wife, friend, and lieutenant to now an inspiration.

That date also serves as a promise to me of *memento mori,* that someday, I, too, will leave this earth, but I will do it emulating Val, living fiercely and wholeheartedly. Finally, the last line holds the all-important motto that sustained her through every challenge: "adapt and overcome." The motto continues to push me through every challenge I confront. It was Val that I thought of during the mental and physical stress of training and during my graduation as I was commissioned as a second lieutenant.

In 2022, I start my military pilot journey in the same state where Val earned her wings. Something I believe she had a hand in. I continue to draw inspiration and strength from her and her memory. Each time I take to the skies, I will never be alone, I will have an angel on the flight deck with me.

My wings are for Val.

Adapt and overcome,

Second Lieutenant Destry S. Jacobs,
USAF

## ACKNOWLEDGMENTS

We would like to thank, first and foremost, Val's family. To her parents, Doreen Cappelaere and Patrice Cappelaere, we could not have created this book without you. Thank you for raising such a courageous and inspiring daughter. Thank you, Caroline Desroches, Val's older sister, and Allison Righter, Val's younger sister. We can't imagine anyone doing more to honor their sister in such big ways. To Carolyn Drake, Val's beloved grandmother, you fostered Val's love of song and her penchant for fashionable clothing. She loved you dearly. To Sean Delaney, Val's husband, you show every day what love looks like for the rest of us.

Thank you to the Wings for Val "Officer Corps." You gave the content for the book and paved the way to this moment. We are so grateful to each and every one of you for sharing your compassion, holding space to learn about Val, befriending her throughout her life and after, volunteering for the organization, sharing our mission, and continuing to honor Val today. These include but are not limited to: John Craighill, Courtney Vandament Callahan, Erin Rawlick Delaney, Destry Jacobs, Daria Malan, Tony Marshall, Jenny Moore, Cecilia Paizs, Andrea Phipps, Mia Stender, Jonathan Stevenson, Danielle Thiriot, and Becky Watson.

We extend our gratitude to the Wings for Val "Flight Crew," the Shadow Ridge School (Hesperia, California) students who encountered Val's incredible story, stepped up, and helped to create this manuscript: Miranda Agapay

Bejarano, Devina Antonellis, Amy Bojorquez Reel, Citlali Cruz, Mia Garcia, Luzaurora Maldonado, Gabriela Martinez, Cynthia Smith . . . and their faculty advisers Principal Olga Fisher and teachers Barbara Jacobs (English), and Jim Hoffmann (Social Studies).

Thank you, Jackie Ruiz, Izar Olivares, and the whole crew at Fig Factor Media, LLC for helping to polish this rough gem of a manuscript into the bright and inspiring book it has become!

## ABOUT THE WINGS FOR VAL FOUNDATION

Navy Lieutenant Valerie Cappelaere Delaney of Anacortes, Washington, served as an EA-6B Prowler student pilot in Electronic Attack Squadron 129 at Naval Air Station Whidbey Island, Washington.

From her humble beginning, Val blossomed into a woman of huge significance. Her military achievements include the Navy Achievement Medal, the National Defense Service Medal and the Global War on Terrorism Service Medal, among others.

Although she lived a short life, only twenty-six years, Valerie's impact was felt during her lifetime and continues to be felt today. She remains a source of inspiration to aviators, and to women around the globe.

The Wings for Val Foundation was formed as a nonprofit organization in 2015 to honor the legacy of Navy fighter pilot Lieutenant Valerie Cappelaere Delaney, who perished during a low-level training mission on March 11, 2013.

The Wings for Val Foundation hopes "to promote and support women pursuing careers in aviation, and to inspire future generations of female leaders to spread their wings and let their dreams take flight," according to the Wings for Val Foundation's Mission.

The Wings for Val Foundation provides scholarships to young women pursuing ambitious careers in aviation. At the time of publication, Wings for Val had given twenty-nine scholarships worth more than $100,000 and plans to continue offering scholarships well into the future.

To help Val's cause, Wings for Val asks you to please share this book, and/or Val's story with a friend. If you would like to donate your time, money, or both, please contact WingsforVal.org for more information.

In the final analysis, it's all about the future of these magnificent young women . . . which is Val's legacy. Will you help these young people to "adapt and overcome?"

Val in the cockpit of a T-34 Turbo Mentor
(Photo credit: Pete Lutz f/6.3 Studio.)

*What are you waiting for?*
*Adapt and overcome!*

# SOURCES

- 4 News Now (Aaron Luna Reporting). "Navy Investigation into Prowler Crash Underway." YouTube, March 12, 2013. Retrieved June 18, 2021: https://www.youtube.com/watch?v=x6fzowLO_iI.
- 4 News Now (Jeff Humphrey Reporting). "Navy: Pilot Error Led to Loss of EA-6B Prowler Near Odessa." YouTube, March 12, 2014. Retrieved June 17, 2021: https://www.youtube.com/watch?v=93ZtOlAGoEo.
- 4 News Now. "Three Believed Dead in Navy Prowler Crash in Lincoln County." YouTube, March 12, 2013. Retrieved June 18, 2021: https://www.youtube.com/watch?v=N6c6LsXGdVE.
- ABC 7 News—WJLA (Robert Lyles Reporting). "Lieutenant Valerie Cappelaere Delaney Killed in Jet Crash." YouTube, March 13, 2013. Retrieved June 14, 2021: https://www.youtube.com/watch?v=0izLk2wIFl8.
- Agarwal, Shivam. "Dale Carnegie is Long Dead, But He Still Can Change Your Life." Medium.com, August 25, 2020.
- AmericanFallenSoldiers.com. "A Tribute to Navy Lieutenant Valerie Delaney." YouTube, July 28, 2014. Retrieved June 18, 2021: https://www.youtube.com/watch?v=OrfGV6Zoo_Y.

- Bandy, Deborah, et al. "Deborah Bandy." Aero Crew News, 27 Feb. 2019, www.aerocrewnews.com/monthly-features/special-features/wings-for-val/.
- Bote, Joshua. "'Get in Good Trouble, Necessary Trouble': Rep. John Lewis in His Own Words." USA Today, July 19, 2020. Retrieved September 4, 2021: https://www.usatoday.com/story/news/politics/2020/07/18/rep-john-lewis-most-memorable-quotes-get-good-trouble/5464148002/.
- Cappelaere, Doreen. "Questionnaire Response." Wings for Val Book—Initial Contact, Barbara Jacobs (via Google Forms), 2019.
- Cappelaere, Patrice. "Questionnaire Response." Wings for Val Book—Initial Contact, Barbara Jacobs (via Google Forms), 2019.
- Cappelaere, Patrice. "This is Not a Eulogy . . ." May 18, 2013. Original is in the possession of the Cappelaere Family.
- Cappelaere, Valerie A., and Joseph P. Unruh. "Experiencing 'Aguerrissement.'" Shipmate, 2008, pp. 16–19.
- Cappelaere, Valerie. "Valerie Cappelaere." Speech to Congregation. July 4, 2010, Corpus Christi, St. Mark's Episcopal Church.
- Cappelaere, Valerie. Various handwritten correspondences in the possession of the Cappelaere Family.
- CHS.HCPSS.org (Centennial High School)

- CollegeConfidential.com. "Do They Come Home?" Talk.CollegeConfidential.com, August 2009. Retrieved September 22, 2021: https://talk.collegeconfidential.com/t/do-they-come-home/736785.
- Craighill, John. "Questionnaire Response." Wings for Val Book—Initial Contact, Barbara Jacobs (via Google Forms), 2019.
- Darney, Caroline. "Remembering LTJG Valerie Cappelaere Delaney." Inside Lacrosse, www.insidelacrosse.com/article/remembering-ltjg-valerie-cappelaere-delaney/18477.
- Das, Andrew. "US Women's Players and US Soccer Settle Equal Pay Lawsuit." The New York Times, February 22, 2022. Retrieved February 27, 2022: https://www.nytimes.com/2022/02/22/sports/soccer/us-womens-soccer-equal-pay.html.
- DayoftheWeek.org
- Delaney, Erin. "Questionnaire Response." Wings for Val Book—Initial Contact, Barbara Jacobs (via Google Forms), 2019.
- Delaney, Sean, and Cappelaere Family. "Valerie Cappelaere Delaney '09." Shipmate, 2013, pp. 168.
- Desroches, Caroline. "Questionnaire Response." Wings for Val Book—Initial Contact, Barbara Jacobs (via Google Forms), 2019.
- Earhart, Amelia. "Quotes." AmeliaEarhart.com. https://www.ameliaearhart.com/quotes/.
- "Eulogy for Valerie Cappelaere" by various friends

and family as read by Daria Malan at the memorial. St. John's Episcopal Church, Ellicott City, Maryland, May 18, 2013.
- "Fairchild Air Force Base, Washington, A History." Weather Underground, www.wunderground.com/history/daily/KSKA/date/2013-3-11?req_city=Harrington&req_state=WA&req_statename=Washington&reqdb.zip=99134&reqdb.magic=1&reqdb.wmo=99999.
- Find A Grave. "Lieutenant Valerie Alice Cappelaere Delaney." Retrieved June 18, 2021: www.findagrave.com/memorial/106819198/valerie-alice-delaney.
- Fire, Color. "Life at the USNA, What Is It Like?" Naval Bagels, March 16, 2018, navalbagelsinc.com/life-at-the-usna-what-is-it-like/.
- Fritze, John. "Naval Academy Graduate from Howard County Killed in Jet Crash." Baltimoresun.com, March 13, 2013. Retrieved June 18, 2021: www.baltimoresun.com/maryland/bs-md-valerie-cappelaere-delaney-20130312-story.html.
- Fowler, Brittanie. "Candace Parker Interview: 'The Hardest Thing I've Had to Overcome . . .'" SwishAppeal.com, January 15, 2016. Retrieved September 21, 2021: https://www.swishappeal.com/2016/1/15/10774092/candace-parker-interview-wnba-title-family-pat-summitt.
- From Staff Reports. "Three Confirmed Dead in Navy Plane Crash Near Harrington." Spokesman.com,

March 14, 2013. Retrieved June 18, 2021: www.spokesman.com/stories/2013/mar/11/naval-plane-crashes-harrington/.
- Glee, Season 6, Episode 5, January 30, 2015, Ryan Murphy Productions, et al.
- Madam CJ Walker. "Madam CJ Walker Quotes." Brainyquotes.com, date unknown, https://www.brainyquote.com/authors/madam-c-j-walker-quotes. For further reading, check out A'Lelia Bundles' masterpiece about Walker, On Her Own Ground (Scribner, 2001).
- Majumdar, Dave and Lagrone, Sam. "2013 Prowler Crash That Killed Three Found to be Result of 'Pilot Error.'" News.USNI.org, March 12, 2014. Retrieved June 22, 2021: https://news.usni.org/2014/03/12/2013-prowler-crash-killed-three-found-result-pilot-error.
- Malan, Daria. "Questionnaire Response." Wings for Val Book—Initial Contact, Barbara Jacobs (via Google Forms), 2019.
- MarkGuerrero.com
- Marshall, Tony, Lieutenant Colonel (retired), Analysis and Interpretation of Official US Navy Report ("Command Investigation") of Mishap (via Zoom), January 16, 2022 (Length 1:13:58).
- Medrut, Flavia. "25 Michael Jordan Quotes That Are Ingredients for Success." Goalcast.com, February 11, 2020. Retrieved September 21, 2021: https://www.goalcast.com/2020/02/11/michael-jordan-quotes/.

- Mission Barbecue. "Stories of Service | Valerie Cappelaere." YouTube, June 29, 2020. Retrieved June 18, 2021: https://www.youtube.com/watch?v=8IQJ_SYjVKo.
- Moore, Jenny. "Questionnaire Response." Wings for Val Book—Initial Contact, Barbara Jacobs (via Google Forms), 2019.
- Morrison, Aaron. "Most Diverse 'Plebes' Arrive at US Naval Academy." Associated Press, July 1, 2009. Retrieved September 22, 2021: http://www2.readingeagle.com/article.aspx?id=146406.
- NMHSchool.org.
- PeriscopeFilm. "The Job of the EA-6B Prowler Grumman Aviation Film 81802." YouTube, July 28, 2015.
- Quintanilla, Selena. Official Twitter Account. May 26, 2018.
- Righter, Allison. "Female Fighter Pilots Teach Us to Spread Our Wings" (TedxLeonardtown). YouTube, October 23, 2017. Retrieved June 14, 2021: https://www.youtube.com/watch?v=GRKY-PXqm-0.
- Righter, Allison. "Questionnaire Response." Wings for Val Book—Initial Contact, Barbara Jacobs (via Google Forms), 2019.
- Stender, Mia. "Questionnaire Response." Wings for Val Book—Initial Contact, Barbara Jacobs (via Google Forms), 2019.
- Stevenson, Jonathan. "Questionnaire Response." Wings for Val Book—Initial Contact, Barbara Jacobs (via Google Forms), 2019.

- STMARKSCC.com
- Tanner, Lindsey. "Officials Find Child-Torture Case 'Abominable'. . .". Los Angeles Times, February 18, 1990.
- Taylor, Phil. "Navy Lieutenant Valerie Delaney" (presented May 23, 2014 to family). The American Fallen Soldiers Project. Retrieved June 14, 2021: https://americanfallensoldiers.com/navy-lt-valerie-delaney/. Taylor's moving work honoring American veteran heroes can be seen at his website AmericanFallenSoldiers.com.
- Travis Manion Foundation. "Lieutenant Valerie Cappelaere Delaney, USN." Facebook: March 11, 2019. Retrieved June 14, 2021: https://www.facebook.com/TravisManionFoundation/videos/lt-valerie-cappelaere-delaney-usn/2008110362572038/.
- TravisManion.org (Valerie Cappelaere Delaney tribute page).
- US Naval Academy Alumni Association. "Last Call" (Shipmate—75th Anniversary Edition). USNA.com, July-August 2013, p. 168.
- US Naval Academy Parents' Club of Northern California, "Info by Class (0-9)," US Naval Academy. Retrieved October 16, 2021: http://usna-nocalparents.org.
- US Naval Academy, "Summer Internships for USNA Midshipman." USNA.edu, https://www.usna.edu/AcResearch/Internships-for-Midshipmen/index.php.

- US Department of Defense. "First Day Midshipman Stand at Attention While Reading Reef Points." June 29, 2005. Retrieved September 22, 2021: https://www.defense.gov/Multimedia/Photos/igphoto/2001243441/.
- "US Women's Soccer Team Files Gender Discrimination Lawsuit." Washington Post, June 5, 2019 (via Newsela). Retrieved June 21, 2021: newsela.com/read/USWNT-equal-pay/id/52608/?utm_source=aotd&utm_medium=email&utm_campaign=test-1&utm_content=news-1.
- Valcourt, Derek. "Family Members Mourn Loss of Howard County Pilot Killed in Navy Jet Crash." CBSLocal.com, March 13, 2013. Retrieved June 18, 2021: baltimore.cbslocal.com/2013/03/13/family-mourns-howard-co-pilot-killed-in-navy-jet-crash/.
- Vandament, Courtney. "Val's Legacy." WingsForVal.org, July 24, 2013.
- W4VBlog.com (Wings for Val Foundation Blog).
- "Welcome to the US Naval Academy Alumni Association & Foundation." USNA.com (US Naval Academy Alumni Association and Foundation). Retrieved June 18, 2021: www.usna.com/tributes-and-stories-in-memoriam-post-9-11-2001.
- "What Is Photorefractive Keratectomy (PRK)?" American Academy of Ophthalmology, July 16, 2018, www.aao.org/eye-health/treatments/photorefractive-keratectomy-prk.

- Whidbey News Times. "More Than 1,200 Attend Memorial Honoring NAS Whidbey Aircrew." WhidbeyNewsTimes.com, March 21, 2013. Retrieved June 18, 2021: www.whidbeynewstimes.com/news/more-than-1200-attend-memorial-honoring-nas-whidbey-aircrew/.
- Wikipedia: Beechcraft T-34 Mentor, Dale Carnegie, Eastern Washington, Harrington, Washington, Line-Crossing Ceremony, McDonnell Douglas T-45 Goshawk, Plebe Summer, Selena, United States Naval Aviator.
- Wings for Val Foundation. "About the Wings for Val Foundation." YouTube, July 29, 2017. Retrieved June 18, 2021: https://www.youtube.com/watch?v=5aPgsvmAHe0.
- Wings for Val—Initial Contact Survey.
- WMAR-2 News (Jeff Hager Reporting). "Navy Pilot from Maryland in Jet Crash." YouTube, March 13, 2013. Retrieved June 17, 2021: https://www.youtube.com/watch?v=udLsyFQjxLE.
- WMAR-2 News (Linda So Reporting). "Naval Officer from Howard County Killed in Crash." YouTube: March 14, 2013. Retrieved June 18, 2021: https://www.youtube.com/watch?v=QHJvDNf4GOI.

www.ingramcontent.com/pod-product-compliance
Lightning Source LLC
Chambersburg PA
CBHW071147060526
44107CB00133B/339